LANDING PLACES

First published in 2010 by
The Dedalus Press
13 Moyclare Road
Baldoyle
Dublin 13
Ireland

www.dedaluspress.com

Editor: Pat Boran

ISBN 978 1 906614 22 5 (bound)
ISBN 978 1 906614 21 8 (paper)

Dedalus Press titles are represented in North America by
Syracuse University Press, Inc., 621 Skytop Road,
Suite 110, Syracuse, New York 13244,
and in the UK by
Central Books, 99 Wallis Road, London E9 5LN

Cover image copyright © Paul Maddern

The Dedalus Press receives financial assistance from
The Arts Council / An Chomhairle Ealaíon

LANDING PLACES

Immigrant Poets in Ireland

EDITED AND INTRODUCED BY

Eva Bourke
&
Borbála Faragó

DEDALUS PRESS

DUBLIN, IRELAND

ACKNOWLEDGEMENTS

The editors would like to acknowledge the support of the Irish Research Council for the Humanities and Social Sciences, and the Spanish Ministerio de Ciencia e Innovación through the project *Us and Them: Discourses on Foreignness by Irish and Galician Women Writers* (1980-2007) (Ref. FFI2009-08475/FILO). We are also extremely grateful to Pat Boran, who agreed so readily to publish this anthology. Owing to his generosity and willingness the project took off at speed. We would also like to thank one of our contributors, Paul Maddern, for his wonderful cover photograph. Thanks are due to those who put us in contact with some poets who had not been aware of our project and also to Anne Fogarty, Andrew Carpenter, Luz Mar González-Arias, Clíodhna Carney, Christiane Schönfeld and Rachel McNicholl for their encouragement and friendship, as well as Máire Ní Annracháin for her help with the Irish language. The invaluable support of our respective husbands Eoin and Tadhg, and our children Gabriel, Miriam, Benjamin and Lorka, Liadh, Imre has made this project fly. In addition, we would like to express our gratitude to all the immigrant poets who entrusted us with their work.

Acknowledgements are also due to the editors of the following in which some of these poems or versions of them originally appeared: Annamaria Crowe Serrano's poem 'Divers' originally appeared in *Femispheres* (Shearsman, UK, 2008). The original Spanish language version of 'Bamboo Time' by Julia Piera was published in *Puerto Rico Digital* (Bartleby Editores, 2009) while the original of 'Self-Portrait of the Invisible Woman' by the same author appeared in *Al vértice de la arena* (Biblioteca Nueva, 2003). Where poems in this anthology have been included in other publications since the time of their submission, the publisher undertakes to acknowledge such publications in future editions on receipt of written advice from the editors.

Finally, thanks to Wake Forest University Press for permission to quote lines from Harry Clifton's poem 'Coming Home' *(Secular Eden: Paris Notebooks 1994—2004*, published 2007) as the epigraph to this anthology.

To Our Hyphenated Families

CONTENTS

Introduction / xvii

INTRODUCTION

"Together we will renew the face of this extraordinary
emerging new Ireland."
—President of Ireland, Mary McAleese

A
s its subtitle suggests, *Landing Places* is an anthology of immigrant poets living in Ireland. Of course it is not accidental that we, as editors, should be interested in and absorbed by the work of such writers since it touches upon our own personal lives. Both of us are ourselves immigrants to this country, and both of us are poets. Both of our families have a narrative of displacement, emigration, religious and political persecution reflecting centuries of a European history of war, expulsions, racism and ethnic cleansing. We know that, whether voluntary or forced, it is never easy to end one life and begin another elsewhere, leaving family and friends, one's familiar places and the sounds of one's language behind.

Roughly twenty years lie between our arrival dates in this country, during which time Ireland underwent such a dizzying and fundamental transformation that the difference in time might as well have been half a century. In the late 1970s EU membership was new, and when people talked about France or Germany, for example, they would use the term "Europe" to make it clear that they didn't quite believe that Ireland was part of that geographical entity. Ireland seemed very remote still from the rest of Europe. You realized you had arrived at the furthest end of the continent when, for instance, you wanted to call family or friends somewhere in Europe. At that time not many people had phones and, as Eva recalls, you either had to book a booth for foreign calls in the post office or collect as many five pence coins as you could hold in your hand, slotting them at the behest of the operator into a black iron box usually to be found in the hallway of a pub. As soon as the operator thought the required sum had been paid—it was a mystery how he knew, whether he actually counted each coin clanking into the box—he then instructed you to press button B and you were connected. It was a lengthy operation and took even longer if you dropped some of the coins. Leaving the island meant booking ferries and trains with ill-matched schedules, long car journeys or the occasional expensive flight. Foreigners were few and far between and almost exclusively of European or American origin. Hundreds of thousands of young, well-educated people were forced to emigrate from Ireland during those years. It was a country in paralysis, deeply insular and inward-looking. But paradoxically, it was inter-connected with the rest of the world through its emigrants.

Perhaps this memory of connectedness has contributed to the relative tolerance and openness of the Irish towards people from outside. In the mid-nineties, when Borbála arrived, Ireland still presented an overwhelmingly "white" face in its city streets and even more strikingly in the country-side, despite the beginnings of the Tiger prosperity. Coming from Hungary, a country which had just started to awaken to life after communism, Ireland seemed oddly familiar in its apparent lack of Western-European self-assurance and people generally seemed very eager to establish common ground. However, Dublin was still a lonely place for a foreigner, where after every introduction people would ask "when are you going home?" There were very few Hungarians or East Europeans here at the time, and most of the Irish, still used to emigration, seemed to find the idea of immigration slightly perplexing. (Why would you want to live here?)

Life has changed dramatically in the last decade, both for the better and for the worse. In the age of broadband, mobile phones, cheap air travel and traffic jams on the M50 at six in the morning it is occasionally hard to recall the Ireland of past decades. But it was not only faster communication channels and much closer cohesion with Europe which have contributed to changing the face of this country but first and foremost the immigrants who have settled here, especially those of the more recent wave of immigration from the accession states and from Africa, Asia, and South America.

Whether the newcomers are "economic" migrants or political refugees, they have begun to put down roots in their communities, their children attend the schools, colleges and universities, and it is to be hoped that nothing will make them feel that they have to uproot themselves again, the recent economic crisis notwithstanding. It is as though overnight Ireland has become ethnically heterogeneous like any other European country, as a glance at the names underneath photographs of school classes or children's sports teams in the local papers will clearly show. And what is more, the presence of these immigrants means an enormous enrichment for Irish life. They have brought their ingenuity with them, their particular sensibility and native wit, their music, language, religion, traditions and last but not least their poetic imagination.

The original plan for this anthology was hatched a little less than a year ago by one of the editors, who then made contact with and proposed it to the other. There followed countless emails, telephone conversations and hours spent reading, discussing and selecting the poems: we are delighted now to present the result— a generous, varied collection of work by sixty-six immigrant poets who have settled in Ireland.

In framing the original request for submissions, we had two principal objectives in mind: the anthology was to reflect the increasing diversity of cultural life in this country and to give people who were born outside of Ireland and came to live here—as well as those who were born here of non-Irish parentage—an opportunity to showcase their distinctive contribution to contemporary Irish writing.

At the beginning of the process of collecting material we had no idea that our call for submissions would meet with such an overwhelming response, from such diverse backgrounds. It is well known that there have been several separate, distinctive waves of immigration to Ireland in the last three to four decades. First there were the refugees who had been offered a home by the Irish state at a time of political persecution and duress—for example Chileans and Boat People from Vietnam during the seventies, and a number of Bosnians who had fled from the war in the Balkans during the nineties. In addition to these "official" immigrant groups there was a loose scattering of individuals who had come to live in Ireland of their own accord for a variety of reasons in the decades prior to the Celtic Tiger, mostly from the United States, Britain and Western Europe. Among our contributors a number of familiar names turned up who belonged to this latter group; they had previously been published in literary magazines and/or book form and were what one might call hyphenated poets, Irish-American, Irish-German, Irish-Russian. They had become assimilated, or "Irishised/Hibernicised". We expected that they would be easier to contact than those belonging to the most recent wave of immigrants who arrived during the Celtic Tiger years of the mid/late nineties onwards.

Ireland's economic boom during that period brought unprecedented levels of prosperity and, for the first time in its history, Ireland experienced a significant inflow of migrants—both workers and asylum seekers—from outside of the European Union. Ireland responded with three new policies. First, to slow down the process, the Irish government created a list of priority-countries when dealing with asylum applications, excluding certain others from consideration. Second, there was a highly significant change in the country's citizenship laws when, after the 2004 referendum, the automatic right to citizenship for the Irish-born children of non-Irish nationals was abolished. Third, Ireland decided in 2004 to allow citizens from the 10 new countries of the EU to work without permits, while at the same time tightening its work-permit system for non-EU applicants, a change which has resulted in a marked increase in Eastern European (mainly Polish) immigration.

The deteriorating economic situation of the post Celtic Tiger era has slowed down the flow of immigration into Ireland, with emigration figures once again on the increase. Currently rising unemployment rates are putting pressure on such immigrant groups, while the danger of discrimination is growing.

In addition to citizens of the accession states of the EU, during this period there was also a significant group of immigrants from various African, Asian, and Latin-American countries, some of whom had applied for political asylum in Ireland. In the initial stages of the editorial process we had been most concerned about reaching this group, but we discovered that many of these people are part of a lively, wide-ranging communications network that includes community groups, writers' workshops[i], libraries and the newspaper publication, *Metro Éireann*. The call for submissions was posted in the "Loose Leaves" column in *The Irish Times*, in *Poetry Ireland Newsletter*, in *Metro Éireann*, as it was also aired on RTÉ and other radio stations and tacked onto countless notice boards in libraries and community groups across the country.

However, the format of this anthology necessarily throws into sharp relief the inevitable constraints of its inclusivity. First of all, we were asking for poems written in the English language, well aware that a large proportion of more recent immigrants probably write in their mother tongue by preference. Aside from the logistical problem of translating poems from a variety of languages within the time-frame we had set ourselves, we also felt that showcasing a poetic appropriation and adaptation of English (and Hiberno-English) merited the present format. (However, as an exception, we included the translated work of Julia Piera, Enríque Juncosa and Andreas Vogel.) In addition, although we advertised in a variety of media and locations, we became aware of the proportionately fewer submissions from certain cultural groups. Within the given limitations, however, while making our selection from the contributions received, we set out to present as large a variety of cultural backgrounds and poetic voices as possible. This anthology therefore is not intended as a sociological survey of resident immigrant groups in the country, neither is it a showcase of all of Ireland's cultural diversity. Rather, it is a window, a glimpse into a sharp and new poetic space produced by the joining, and sometimes collision, of Irish experience and immigrant perspective.

We believe that an anthology of this nature has been rendered even more timely by the current economic crisis. Immigration into Ireland during the Tiger era was made more visible than previously, not only by the numbers who arrived, but also because of skin colour. Although Africans represented a relatively small minority of the immigrants of this period, they attracted a disproportionate amount of negative attention and hostility, which focused most strikingly on the issue of immigrant women coming to Ireland to give birth, leading, arguably, to a referendum to protect the "purity" of Irish citizenship. There are genuine fears that the state's current economic difficulties may lead to further prejudice towards those perceived as non-native. In this context, a recognition of the imaginative achievement of immigrants and their actual and potential contribution to the rich tapestry of Irish cultural life becomes even more important.

Historically, European and American (white) immigrants have been well represented in existing anthologies of Irish literature, although submerged within a homogenised interpretation of Irishness. The rapid changes within Irish society over the last two decades make this approach increasingly problematic, because immigrants, both in number and colour, have come to represent a far more visible group of people with differentiated identities. A persistent tendency at governmental level to demarcate immigrants, asylum-seekers and refugees indistinguishably as not-the-norm ("non-Irish", "non-national", "non-citizen") highlights the need to research immigrant identities within, and outside of, definitions of national identity. Compiling an anthology of immigrant work thus serves a dual purpose of unsettling a normative definition of Irishness on the one hand, and creating a visible space for self-expression on the other.

This work, however, is by no means the first recognition of the immigrant voice in Ireland. Over the past decade, Susan Knight's remarkable collection of interviews with immigrant women, Michael O'Loughlin's anthology of writing from Galway and a significant amount of non-literary research have explored the nature of the "new" Irish experience. However, the current volume offers a particular insight into a burgeoning field of contemporary Irish poetry, which is likely to change the terrain of the Irish literary landscape.

In other European countries with a longer history of immigration, the impulses from immigrant writers have been and continue to be important and transformative for mainstream literature. International examples indicate that a process of cross-fertilisation will take place: the native imagination can profit from the "outsiders'" dual consciousness, from the way they experience and represent their host country and transform their literary medium, while in turn the contact or confrontation with an existing artistic nexus can provide inspiration and material for an immigrant sensibility. (Not only are there excellent immigrant writers in Britain, France and Germany, for example, but also film-makers, musicians, actors, theatre directors, dancers, visual artists and even stand-up comedians.)

In his essay entitled "Coming Home", published in the literary journal *Irish Pages*, Harry Clifton, himself a second generation immigrant poet, writes: "English departments of universities are waiting for the emergence—poetry first, then prose—of a new immigrant literature, the first of its kind in the state, the bittersweet fruits of Chinese, East European and African experience on our soil". Clifton has correctly defined a novel opportunity for research and publications within Irish academia—we believe, however, that this anthology will also find much interested and enthusiastic reception outside university walls. It is highly likely that the next generation, the children of the immigrants, perhaps even of some of our contributors, will go on to help define the imaginative contours of the Irish experience in the coming decades.

As in any anthology, different approaches can be taken to organising the work. Similar volumes from other countries often group their contributions thematically or chronologically. Because *Landing Places* is an introduction to poets from countries as far apart as Japan and Canada, Spain and the US, Poland and India, Germany and South Africa, we have tried to make it as comprehensive and inclusive as possible, without imposing thematic constraints. The poetry therefore is heterogeneous and mixed, just like the contributors themselves. Some of the poets enjoyed the privilege of choice when settling here, others are "forced" immigrants; there are long-term residents and new arrivals among them, Anglophone writers and a variety of language backgrounds, established poets and beginners. This diversity is aptly reflected in the thematic variety presented: there are poems about displacement, home, language, identity, death, love, environment, gender, and more or less any other topic one can think about. We organised our contributors alphabetically and asked them to send us a short biography and a photograph so that readers will be able to gain an insight into the individual immigrant experience and the way it informs or underlies the poems, even if it is not explicitly their theme.

We have arrived, as Harry Clifton says, not at a crossroads, but at a global intersection. This anthology hopes to draw attention to the diverse poetic output of Ireland's immigrant communities and to open the way to similar future ventures. These poetic voices are not marginal, but are at the very heart of what shapes Irishness today. Julia Kristeva calls the foreigner the "hidden face of our identity"—the "other" within us who makes us face our own diversity. Our fruitful cultural co-existence is crucial for the development of an integrated multi-ethnic society within Ireland. The picture that emerges from these poems suggests that there is a strong new cultural space which is occupied by the immigrant imagination. President Mary McAleese's hope that Ireland will become "a common homeland where people can be fully and absolutely themselves and yet share a common future" is manifest in many of these works. In the President's words, together we will renew the face of Ireland.

Eva Bourke and Borbála Faragó
January 2010

LIST OF WORKS

—Clifton, H. (200)"Coming Home" in *Irish Pages* Vol.3, No.2.

—Faragó, B. (2008). "I am the Place in which Things Happen: Invisible Immigrant Women Poets of Ireland" (pp. 145-167) in *Irish Literature: Feminist Perspectives*. Coughlan, P., O'Toole, T. (eds.). Dublin: Carysfort Press.

—Immigrant Council of Ireland. (2003). *Handbook on Immigrants' Rights and Entitlements in Ireland*. Dublin: Immigrant Council of Ireland. Online: http://www.immigrantcouncil.ie/images/3492_handbook2003.pdf

—Knight, S. (2001). *Where the Grass is Greener: Voices of Immigrant Women in Ireland*. Dublin: Oak Tree Press.

—Kristeva, J. (1991). *Strangers to Ourselves*. New York: Columbia University Press. Translated by Leon Roudiez.

—Lentin, R., McVeigh, R. (eds.) (2002). *Racism and Anti-Racism in Ireland*. Belfast: Beyond the Pale Publications Ltd.

—McAleese, M. (2007). "The Changing Faces of Ireland: Migration and Multiculturalism". *British Council Annual Lecture, 14 March, 2007*. Online: http://www.britishcouncil.org/home-about-us-world-of-difference-our-annual-lecture.htm?mtklink=world-of-difference-our-annual-lecture 14/12/2009.

—O'Loughlin, M. (2008). *Galway: City of Strangers*. Galway: Galway City Council Arts Office.

—Ruhs, M., Quinn, E. (2009) "Ireland: from Rapid Immigration to Recession". Online: http://www.migrationinformation.org/USfocus/display.cfm?ID=740 (10/12/09).

—Sheridan, V. (2008) "Loneliness and Satisfaction: Narratives of Vietnamese Refugee Integration Into Irish Society" (pp. 108-122) in Faragó, B. and Sullivan, M. (eds.). *Facing the Other: Interdisciplinary Studies on Race, Gender and Social Justice in Ireland*. Newcastle: Cambridge Scholars Publishing.

[i] See for example Women Writers in the New Ireland Network: http://wwinc.wordpress.com/

And souls come in from the cold, foregatherings,
The still, small voice, unable to hear itself think,

Salvaging, here and there, a living word
From the drift of happenstance,
A soundbite or an anecdote, somebody met by chance,
The key to an inner mystery. Safe, *a bord,*
Between two worlds, suspended in mid-flight,
I dream of a bare table, the warmth to come,
A silence at the heart of Paris, a room,
Detached, anonymous, nothing to do but write.

—*from* 'Coming Home', Harry Clifton

CHRIS AGEE

Chris Agee was born in 1956 in San Francisco and grew up in Massachusetts, New York and Rhode Island. He attended Harvard University and since 1979 has lived in Ireland. He is the author of three books of poems, *In the New Hampshire Woods* (The Dedalus Press, 1992), *First Light* (The Dedalus Press, 2003) and *Next to Nothing* (Salt, 2009), as well as the editor of *Scar on the Stone: Contemporary Poetry from Bosnia* (Bloodaxe, 1998, Poetry Society Recommendation), *Unfinished Ireland: Essays on Hubert Butler* (Irish Pages, 2003) and *The New North: Contemporary Poetry from Northern Ireland* (Wake Forest University Press, 2008). He is currently completing a collection of essays, *Journey to Bosnia*. He reviews regularly for *The Irish Times* and is the Editor of *Irish Pages*, a journal of contemporary writing based at The Linen Hall Library, Belfast. He holds dual Irish and American citizenship, and spends part of each year at his house near Dubrovnik, in Croatia.

Achill Triptych

BOELL'S FUCHSIA
Heinrich Böll

Let's begin, say, with this blow-in from the Japanese Pacific,
windbreak weeping blood-red, globe-empurpled lanterns: exotic

pagodas of the old Irish hedge, companion to hart's-tongue
and flag-iris, the verge's trench and the mossy ditch,

famine's rhododendron, the post-war electrification ...
And let us ask, say, why we would ever need

to find the place of Golgotha if the reality
of textdom—its meaning—give it us already?

O lovely Ireland! writes Hein with irony (fondly). And in
his journal's epilogue: *Honour and glory are due to the Irish*

women who bring such lovely children into the world,
to the Irish tinkers, and to the fuchsia hedges—the same country,

he adds, that gave us *lynch.*
                              Or *boycott.* Still, it's hard squaring
all this downtrodden charm with that cemetery at Letterfrack.

CAMILLE SOUTER ON ACHILL
(Camille Souter)

For me this is the true ideal of the pure artist,
independent spirit at the periphery of everything,

at the centred heart of her singular art. Original
tongue-in-groove, bed, armchair, a hearth, ciggies,

sleeping quarters-cum-parlour, good food off the hob
and not talking shop, keen memory for people and times,

a hatred of selling. On her sward of grass at the back
between white cottage gable and walled studio shed

a barrow of hay, sea-stones, teazle, sculptures, flotsam
and floats, rusted net-weights, a hawser, a boat.

Crocheted cap, green fingers, schoolgirl tales, Turner's
"rum job". Famous Grouse and Guinness. Stay close

to the things that made you. If mainstream, so much
the worse. If not, *tant mieux* at untopical eighty!

ISLANDER
(John F. Deane)

Everything's a path. Nothing's a path. That is the lesson
of the ascent up Slievemore, bog-pools and orchids

at the top; in the distance, the deal boomerang
of Keel Strand, islets in silhouette floating

humpbacked in the offing. Each square metre's full
of the small beauties: speedwell, self-heal, bog-cotton,

innumerable shamrocky tormentil. To say nothing
of heather's mauve-grey, gambolling fritillaries,

spongy sundew and spaugham moss blanketing
the transhumance past at whose existential foot

is the return to *Sean Reilig*, and a clatter of clachans
like a weathered jawbone unroofed by history's root-canal.

ii

Writing's like cooking: it has, and is, the two things,
ingredients and technique, mind and body, ship and anchor,

the inner leaven, the executory act: the language of life,
the life of the language—the world as recipe, your own

personal cuisine; but of the two, that first, deed to word, is
its indispensable necessity to a matching sufficiency.

And here was your first world of first things
in first words in the first place. Darkened, of course,

by those dream-figures of Paul Henry now well
and truly buried at Letterfrack. Your watchword loyalty

against seductions of the centripetal, the other West's
apathetic heart, not your islandman's far-flung, far-out

magnetic West—where once, as H.B. imagined it,
so far from the centre of things, as if it had slipped way out

into the Atlantic, lay the glowing heart of Europe ...
                                                    Young
Daedalus, old artificer indeed—and, indeed, in deed as well.

                                    Heinrich Böll Cottage
                                    Achill Island, Co. Mayo
                                    June 2009

Letterfrack Industrial School Graveyard

Nape, brow, collarbone, hands: suddenly, annoyingly
alive with midges, invasively cloying—a little like
(swift afterthought), in the swampy air, {subset
of the sheughs of the swarming dead, all aswarm

4 ⬧ AGEE

from some *Éire*-land of no-spices}, those social gnats
swatted at, shooed off, shunted away, now under foot
this late Saturday afternoon, midsummer June's wan sunshine
trying to peek through the cloud of Major MacBride's Irish air.

On the way in, a distinct scent of pungent ramson;
zoomorphic ferns, and flag-iris, and mossed beechboles
clambered with ivy. Recent big blowdown
freshly sawn, the *deora Dé* of fuchsia scattered
everywhere. On the way out, a plain woodcross
(two-by-twos) at sea in the Ivy, Flags and Ferns,
at a decent distance, at a "dacent interval," from
the stone sign bearing this little Srebrenica of schoolboys.

And in-between? A blue ceramic Noddy-car plant pot sat
with funny headlamp-eyes on the plinth of their memorial cross.
Unnamed slate-slabs for the seventy-one, now re-marked by
those black heartstones of the-also-institutionalized-religious
propped up to the light. At the other end, coins and kitsch,
flowering plants and a toy truck attached to Blake's
The Garden of Love.
                And why—come to it now—this high ratio of teenagers
to littler ones, or "died as a young boy," in the State's un-shining parish

of corrupted Republic? And come to it too, my hour photographing—
just another Sweeney "bucklepping"?
                        Only on the road back, broken
line passing under, acceleration's hot tracers or short lives,
did the cleric's kick hit me from the gullet to the eyes.

June 2009

PETER OLIVER ARNDS

Peter Oliver Arnds was born in Hannover, Germany, in 1963. After travelling and working in Australia in the early 1990s, where he met Jerrilynn Romano, he pursued a doctoral degree in German Studies at the University of Toronto. From 1995 until 2008 he worked as a Professor of German and Italian at Kansas State University. He has also taught at Colby College, Maine, at Middlebury College, Vermont, and in 2007 at the University of Kabul. In 2008 Peter, his wife Jerrilynn, and their son Jonas came to Dublin where Peter now lectures comparative literature and literary translation at Trinity College Dublin. His research interests are diverse and include German literature and culture, comparative literature, cultural theory, translation and creative writing. A substantial part of his work revolves around human rights, with a focus on genocide and its cultural modes of representation, on memory and migration. Peter continues to write and publish poetry and prose. He has completed a travel book on his romance in Australia, has published in the *Frankfurter Allgemeine Zeitung* about his experience in Afghanistan, and was recently the president of the *Society of Contemporary American Literature in German* (SCALG).

The End of the Celtic Tiger

tiger tiger burning out
what on earth is life about?
is it piling up on high
all the stuff that you can buy?
being busy
gaining fame

Lord Almighty:
I get so dizzy
with that game.

Moth in the Juke Box

A moth had died inside the juke box
At Dean's Café Rushcutter's Bay
I don't know what had been the cause to kill it
Whether the music or just lack of air
But the moth seemed mummified
And must have sat there
Well preserved and over the years
In its glass coffin,
Its wings brittle and white
Trembling ever so slight under the musical vault.

When first we spotted the immortal moth
It squatted on the number ninety-nine:
Herb Alpert's This guy's in love with you,
Which we kept playing
Over chocolate shakes and nacho dips.
But every time on later trips
When I'd be back at Dean's Café
The music had moved the moth
From song to song,
Giving it far beyond its death
An eerie kind of mobility.
The immutable but movable messenger from beyond
Had travelled from Abba to KISS
Up and down the charts
But never back to that one tune
To which since the early days of our love
I had never grown immune.

CELESTE AUGÉ

 Celeste Augé was born in Canada in 1972. She was raised in the backwoods of Northern Ontario until her family moved to Ireland, where she has lived since she was twelve years old. In 2006 she published her first chapbook of poetry, *Tornadoes for the Weathergirl.* Her poetry has also been included in the anthology *The Ground Beneath Her Feet* (Cinnamon Press) and in the chapbook Smoke and Skin (Lapwing). She has been Writer-in-Residence with an after-school programme in Galway, supported by the Arts Council and the National Youth Arts Programme. She has read her work at Cúirt International Festival of Literature, at Galway City & County libraries, at Poetry Ireland's Introductions series of readings, and at other literary events around Ireland. Her poetry was short-listed for a 2008 Hennessy Literary Award. She lives in County Galway.

The Essential Guide to Flight

I've been abandoning a continent slowly,
for twenty-two years now, standing in a room
without language. One step outside
and the weather wraps itself around me,
steals back a loose vowel, the phone number
of my childhood home, whatever it can get away with.

Molly (the Golden Mule)

When I came back, the world smelt
of damp earth and rich fusty sweat.

Suddenly I could stop traffic, press
my friction-hot hooves into the tarmac,
clop across in stubborn time.

My day turned to the sweet focus
of skin on my flank, the rub
of a tourist intent on seeing
the boggy side of the mountain.
Avoiding nettles, the cliff sides.

The colours drew them up there,
perched on my back, each step a wish,
that phantom of brown carved out
against slate blue, the weight of purple
as the heather flared in peat.

Hill of Doon, they would say to me,
over and over, laughing,
their voices booming down the length
of my ears. I would practice the silence
I had learnt between lives.

What I have now: two friends
in the meadow, grass, enough to share.
A strong back and my mother's long legs.
Forget that my father was an ass.
I hide my own traits and turns,

a dangerous liking for sugar highs,
that fermenting in my bloodstream.
Haunted by an odd chromosome,
my spine holds one body at a time,
on the outside. A quiet connection.

So why shouldn't I take care of myself,
refuse to work past what I can capably do?
Why should I pitch my fierce back
into the ditch when I can stand proud,
ready to shoulder enormous dreams.

Footfall

Our shadows stretch ahead of us.
The cool November yellow
reminds us of Florian's feast day,
the way we can laugh at anything.
I carry her handbag, wonder at how
such a small vessel can weigh
so much, how such a small shoulder
can carry this much around,
footfall after footfall, and I promise
to take her to the first coffee shop
I can find after we call to the church,
check the notices and add our own—
looking for work, good English,
hardworking, optimistic. She kisses
this handwritten sheet for luck then pins it
to the board, leaving behind a piece of her
spirit; and we walk to the next source,
refill ourselves with held hands
and petrol station coffee.

The steam swirls between cold
and the next day of work, and we step
over that low wall, leave the forecourt,
laugh at the sight of a fully robed monk
who carries a sign for the last

pizzeria before Oughterard,
and we can't even pronounce
that place, but we laugh anyway,
that early morning tickle laugh that lasts
all day when the woman you love
is holding your hand and you can't see
past the length of your shadow
on a low-sun day in Galway in November,
when you can't see the long grey days
that will pull down the winter,
the way the rain will get everywhere
and black streets turn grey, slick
with rain, thinking you're strong
and can walk all day.

DENISE BLAKE

Denise Blake was born in Ohio, U.S.A in 1958. Her family moved back to Co. Donegal in 1969. Her first selection of poetry, *Take a Deep Breath*, was published by Summer Palace Press and a second collection is due in 2010. Her work is included in *The Echoing Years*, an anthology of poetry from Canada and Ireland. She has contributed to *Sunday Miscellany* RTÉ Radio 1 and her work is included in the *Sunday Miscellany* anthologies. She was shortlisted for the Sunday Tribune/Hennessy for a first short story. She read at Out to Lunch readings at the Bank of Ireland Arts Centre, Dublin and read as part of CLÉ Author and Publisher library tour. Her work has been published in *The SHOp, Poetry Ireland Review* , *The Stinging Fly* and *West 47*. She is a founder of the Errigal Writers' Group and she received an MA in poetry from Lancaster University through the Poets' House.

Migration

Swallows fly in low swoops around me
as I try to mow straight patterns across our lawn.
Ten, maybe twelve, arcing their own flight path
like speed skaters weaving through a packed rink.

Last week our son, home on holidays, mowed
this same patch and already his mark has disappeared.
On the morning of his leaving a mallard marched up
the grass slope towards our home, her seven ducklings

waddled in a tight line behind her, like pre-school children
on an outing. Eyeing us, she about-faced. The row rippled

away down the hill towards the lake. By what instinct
did they know that this man-made lake existed?

And what instinct makes our young want to fly away?
I only know as he headed to departure, long shorts, flip-flops
and a polo top—already looking like a New Englander—
I understood what it is to be heartsore.

The lawnmower tries to run off down the hillock,
I'm leaving a very shaky pattern behind me.
A grey heron comes flying from the River Lennon, crash-lands
into the centre of the lake. What has led him to this place?

Letterkenny 567

The black phone didn't have a dial,
just a small side-handle to crank.
Number please?
Letterkenny 32.
The operator might say, *No point ringing there,*
they are all away for the day.
If you did get through there was a tick-tick
like a cricket in a night-forest.
Someone was listening.

Words came at me in swarms of locusts.
Chips were crisps. French fries were chips.
Jelly was jam. Jello was jelly.
No one knew what pizza was.
It wasn't only pizza we had left behind,
but clothes in psychedelic patterns.
There, I had worn the phone as an earring
while having endless talks full of baloney.

They didn't have baloney here, but spam;
apple-pie sweets and gobstoppers.
I needed a lot of those.
Never asked the right questions:
Where does your Father work?
Never gave the right answers:
Yes. I do miss Cleveland.

You couldn't just ring Cleveland.
Calls were as sacred as Our Lady.
Neighbours came to our house
for urgent messages, left coins beside the phone.
And when I did make a local call;
Don't talk too long.
You're not in America now.

MEGAN BUCKLEY

 Megan Buckley was born in New York in 1977, and has lived in Ireland since 2004. Her poems have been published in the US, the UK, and Ireland, in publications such as *The Ledge* (US), *The Pedestal* (US), *eclectica.org* (US); the 'Dazzle and Attract' Project in Newcastle-on-Tyne, UK, in which one of her poems was projected onto the wall of a building (UK); *Crannog* (IRL), and others. She has presented her work at the Over The Edge Showcase at the Cúirt International Festival of Literature in April 2008, and was a judge for the Cúirt Poetry Grand Slam in 2009. Buckley is currently a Doctoral Teaching Fellow in the English Department at NUI, Galway, where she teaches seminars on nineteenth-century women's poetry.

Seventh son of a seventh son

In a September night in a concrete kennel,
in the presence of a dozen baying greyhounds,
we watch him work. You lean against the wall,
I perch on a dirty upturned bucket.
For once, you are silent.

We watch him hold each dog between his legs,
see him divine where the problem lies
in each lithe body—spine, paw, knee, joint;
he feels the error with his fingers,
then, with his butcher's grip, he twists
the pain into each animal and out again.
You and I learn the art of reticence, so unnatural to us both;
we learn to hold our breaths together.

We learn that he effs and blinds while he works,
grunts punctuated with "fuck"s;
we learn that healing is guttural,
all dirt and sacrifice,
and that dogs scream in human voices when they suffer.

Later, you tell me he is proud, but I tell you he is humble;
it took years to realign the clean bones
of his own life to accommodate the healer's curse.
Now, at forty, the physician cannot heal himself;
the animal aches have pushed him far into old age.
And you and I, amid the smell of hurt and fur,
learn our own craft of the hands;
to let the suffering come.

Climbing

We started in Ballyvaughn,
when all the craft shops were shut
for January, when the sun burns itself out
in six hours. We made for the Burren,
you spanning the land with your giant's legs,
and me trotting along beside,
an eager cocker spaniel. You walked; I ran.

We made it to the top of the mountain (you
called it a hill); rain threatened, but the flood
never came; just a curve of rainbow, the arc of the
covenant. You promised, *I know exactly how*
to get back down, and then jumped the whole way
from rock to rock. It began to hail then, and midway
you waited for me, laughing, covered in sweat and hail
and cowshit, dotted with blood from a scrape on my right hand.

Finally, at the bottom,
you lifted me through a thicket of briars, and I stepped
out onto the road, the mountain rising behind us, silent;
a dream we had, a past life, a headstone for a journey's end.
I never saw the Burren, not then or any afternoon;
but all that time it had lain waiting for us, with its moon-
and tooth-scapes, its cattle tracks. Only you had seen it,
with your geographer's eye, your feel for things invisible,
your enviable faith.

SANDRA BUNTING

Sandra Bunting was born in 1953 in Colorado Springs, USA, the daughter of a Canadian journalism protégé of Lord Beaverbrook and an RCAF intelligence officer on loan for a year to NORAD. Shortly after her birth, Sandra moved back with her parents to Canada. She went on to live in many provinces but always spent summers at Burnt Church, New Brunswick. Because of her Irish ancestry on her mother's side, she started a correspondence with the Irish Embassy in what happened to be the 50th anniversary of the 1916 rising. The next year she convinced her mother to move to Dublin and witnessed the beginning of 'The Troubles' in the North. Back in Canada, after graduating from Toronto's Ryerson in Radio and Television Arts, Sandra worked in the news department of the Canadian Broadcasting Corporation. On a leave of absence she met her Irish husband in Spain, married in 1988 and moved to Galway. Sandra has dual citizenship: Canadian and Irish. She is currently on the editorial board of *Crannóg* magazine. Her poetry collection *Identified in Trees* was published in 2006 by Marram Press. Some of her poems are in the permanent collection of the Galway museum. She also works in printmaking, batik and book binding and has had her work exhibited in Galway, Sligo and Montreal. She lives in Galway City with her two daughters and a Cairn Terrier.

Fragments

I admit I've kept things from you,
packed them away
where you could not find them.
I fed you bits, crumbling the rest,

dry leaves in my hand
to keep you in the dark,
shield you from the battles
and meanness of my age.

How far back do we have to go
to dislodge secrets of the past?
Can we ever know for sure?

It is no harm to think you
come from a line of kings
yet you say you have to know me
to understand yourself.
I become the answer
to your questions.
You do not see me scramble
to search the past in slivers.

Exile

My home is among rocks now.
Rain pellets beat time on glass
as morning sun tries to come out.

A dancer in the window moves
parts of her body in isolation.
Over a convent wall, a donkey brays.

Stones look out like little men.
I stand alone away from my land
of snow, tall trees and frozen sea.

From the drizzled grass and limestone,
childish voices call me to look at daffodils,
a little hand takes mine, keeping me here.

Canadian Mother Moves to Dublin in '68

Priests shook with fear.
She was confident, Catholic and divorced
and thought nothing of smuggling
birth control pills to Dublin
for newly married neighbours.

Because she was a Bunting,
the postman threw her letters
down in muck at her door.
On a Derry trip, a tour company
changed her name to Evans,
for her protection, they said,
but a musicologist from the north
caught her out. She had Catholic eyes.

Images of her namesake flicker:
carrying a cudgel, riding a white horse.
It seemed a long way from Canada.
Like walking into the past, she said,
but she wanted to stay.
It was easier than going home.

KRISTINA CAMILLERI

 Kristina Camilleri is a young writer and student of philosophy. She was born in Los Angeles, California in 1988 and lived there until 1998 when her parents, immigrants from Malta, decided to return to the island. A decade later, and having completed an initial year at the University of Malta, Kristina decided to look for opportunities abroad, moving to Ireland where she lived in Drogheda for the next eight months.

Immigrant

October, Ireland
the sun pierces holes
through our agenda
we no longer see
what we thought

in today's true light,
we see true dirt

we find out
we are not them, either
and we will move on, out

with hope to find
cleaner light elsewhere,
cleaner sun,
as all land is dirt

ANAMARIA CROWE SERRANO

 Anamaría Crowe Serrano was born in Dublin, where she currently lives, though her childhood was divided between the school year in Co. Meath and the rest of the year in Spain. Her father, Peter Crowe, comes from a long line of stonemasons whose sculptures and headstones can be seen around Ireland. Her mother, Ana Serrano Bericat, is an accomplished painter, interior decorator and DIY expert. She came to Ireland from her native Zaragoza as a student in the early 1960's to learn English for a few months and stayed for over thirty years. Anamaría has worked as a freelance translator—from Spanish and Italian—for almost twenty years, interspersed with teaching Spanish language at third level and privately. Having worked with a number of different genres, she now concentrates on translating contemporary Italian poetry. Publications of her own work include a collection of short stories, *Dall'altra parte* (Leconte, Rome, 2003) a collaborative poetry project, *Paso Doble* (Empiria, Rome, 2006) with Italian poet Annamaria Ferramosca, and a collection of poetry, *Femispheres* (Shearsman, UK, 2008), from which the poem "Divers" is taken. She is the recipient of two travel awards from the Arts Council of Ireland.

High-wire
after Cesar Vallejo

what is the moment
suspended on a geometry of emotion—
the line between this
          and that
now
   and then

supporting the weight of the walker
one foot rising
cajoling oxygen, hydrogen
the nitric toe
searching blindly for the tension
as vision vibrates

seeing is as useless
as knowing the angles
distances
there is no comfort
in calculation

the foot relies on other armour
on the breath
a balance of spirit
that translates three meters
into applause
the taut rapture of spectacle
and belief, belief
always beyond the physical

the moment is performed
years in advance
long before the foot
has learned to dream

Identity

these words, bricks of babel
stacked in the streets
of my tongue

the syntax wobbles
sounding nothing like the rhapsody
it was meant to be

an architecture of uncertainty
mispronounces the simpler words
sputtering the sibilants
stressing place between plosives

the broken machinery
grinds inside the cranium
murders meaning

my native tongue translates as

relating or belonging to a person or thing

a member of an indigenous people

glottic, lingual

a movable mass of muscular tissue

my native tongue flaps and
clanks, unoiled
abandons me to the gibberish of
a person or thing abstracted
an indigent us
forked and floudering under the weight
of silence

(untitled)

where do streets lead
without a working compass
magnetic north spinning south
unsure of its itinerary

my steps on asphalt
wrongfoot their own cartography
stumble on the failing memory
of wood on quay
dubh in *linn*

the landmarks are of loss
construction begetting
deconstruction, land
no longer a mark of its people
locked in dislocation
       errant
            erring

I take a left turn into silence
clueless
in the sinister side of complicity

Divers

They dive
deep down
the ones who dare
with total trust in oxygen tanks
and the quality of care

that goes into nurturing
something as basic as a breath

They dive for what they find
bubbling between the fissures
of anonymity
grains of sand stirred by fish tails
long-flickered out of sight
shoals of tiny species
gliding en masse
to camouflage weakness—
all the lessons of the world
flowing in semi-darkness and flawless
not the slightest hint of triumph
at their success

They dive to feel the beat
of their own heart, compressed
the rush of knowing they've reached
home in an alien world
where the rules are unknown
therefore unbroken
and the old self is shed
drowning the madness overhead
renewed for a moment
before the air
runs out

KINGA ELWIRA CYBULSKA

 Kinga Elwira Cybulska was born in Poland in 1982, one hundred years after Virginia Woolf. She considers herself as "constantly torn" between Poland and Ireland. In 2006 she received her MA in Polish language and literature. Her work was published in the anthology *Galway: City of Strangers*, edited by Michael O' Loughlin. In 2008 she participated in the Polish Poetry Evening (organized by Over The Edge) and Over The Edge Summer Open-mic. She also attended a couple of Kevin Higgins's poetry workshops at Galway Arts Centre. The main area of her interests includes: "the stream of consciousness", slightly darker sides of human nature, angelology and various kinds of feminism.

Warsaw

A tram meanders slowly to the airport.
I used to look through dusty blinded windows
And I am sighing now. Time is quoting itself.

The road diverged in Warsaw: exquisite greyness.
Always the underground of existence, fame of sorrows.
I am smuggling my books, ginger biscuits, my Master of Arts.
Gaining the bitterness of Guinness and a bite of W B Yeats.
Spitting out the sticky joke of a month's salary.
Over fifty years of systems disguised in glamorous ideas.
I will miss stunning ugliness, crushing leaves with my heels.
Sweet, cold mornings of weakness in November.

The road diverged in Warsaw. It was four o'clock in the morning
In New York and a man enjoyed espresso on his way to work.

I Am Not Going Anywhere

I am not going anywhere. There won't be another day.
Twenty three hours and the memory of snow curled up
Under my skin.
I listened to the city yawning, breathing out buses.
No certainty, rotten fabrics made of the day.

I am not going anywhere. There will be no shadows.
Only shapes formed by the remains of things
In the suitcase.
I touch the glass, it is warm from reflections.
I suffocated once with the thick fog of the morning.

I am not going anywhere. There will be no metropolis.
Just distant, lucid recollections thrown from the sky
In vain.
And the ginger eyes of the city are watching sarcastically.

Dreams and Awakenings

Every night and every morning
Possibilities crawl undefined.

I could have been this girl—
Her face drifting in a puddle of a window
On a night train to Paris.

Or with every anorexic reflection
Living on self-hatred and lettuce.

A mythological sylph in disguise
Giggling viciously outside heaven.

KATHRYN DAILY

 Kathryn Daily was born in Texas in October 1956, and has lived in Europe for over 20 years. For the past 10 years, she has made her home in Letterkenny, County Donegal, with her son, Steven who was born in Dublin. She holds a BA in English from the University of Maryland in Heidelberg, Germany; a Diploma in Women's Studies from UCD; and a postgraduate diploma in Guidance & Counselling from the University of Ulster. A former soldier in the US Army and founding member of Glass Apple Writers, Letterkenny, she is also Chairperson of the Board of Management of Letterkenny Educate Together National School. She works as a costumer and creative writing/arts facilitator. She won first prize in the Charles Macklin Poetry Competition (2001) in both the single poem and collection categories. Her poems were included in *A Deeper Light*, published by Glass Apple Writers, and *Gathering O' The Clans*, an anthology published for the Newtownards Festival of the Peninsulas. She was a winner in the Smurfit Samhain Poetry Competition, Gortahork, County Donegal (2007). Her first collection of poetry, *The Comfort of a Wicked Past*, was published by Summer Palace Press in 2008.

Anniversary

You'd bury me with your people, you said,
dearly wreathed loved ones, Cockhill clay spattered.
Where will I lie now, when your love is dead?

I followed your tannin-stained footsteps—you led.
Like wind-blown seeds my gypsy tribe scattered.
You'd bury me with your people, you said.

Secrets and open wounds yeasted our bread.
My wedding dress dragged, fringed and tattered.
Where will I lie now, when your love is dead?

My hope was a window curtained with lead -
whispered warnings like stinging stones clattered.
You'd bury me with your people, you said.

Rose petal red dripped across our wide bed
when you lay with her, dreaming us shattered.
Where will I lie now, when your love is dead?

Divorced, cast away, yet still I am wed
to homeland lost, relations ungathered.
You'd bury me with your people, you said.
Where will I lie now, when your love is dead?

Penelope Dreams

With each night's unraveling,
I explore the far distant universe
of my past.
Navigating my threaded maze,
I find myself—
one hand clutching a web-strand,
the other gripping my pocketful of crumbs.
Weaving my way home,
I hold fast, as talismans,
the thousand fragile ways
we each attempt,
to keep ourselves
from being lost.

Sojourner

I want to go to Mars.
I want to leave dusty red footprints
to mark the mystery of my passing
for a thousand years
on a landscape
older, drier and more desolate
than me.

Here in this green wet place
I am desiccating,
a brown leaf crumbling on the wind.
I am wasting and wanting.
I want to feel lush, if only by contrast.
I want to go to Mars.

CARLA DE TONA

Carla De Tona was born in the heart of Italy, Umbria, in 1973. She moved to Dublin in 1999 for one year (to attend a master's course), and she has incautiously been there since. In 2007 she completed a PhD on Italian migrant women in Ireland from Trinity College Dublin, where she now works as a researcher. This is her second poem to be published and she never thought she would go this far.

The 20th of September 2006

Day 12,220 of my life. More or less, but still, an impressive
    number.
It is 2515 days today since I came to Dublin.
My friend Frances is leaving tomorrow. I met her 2506 days ago.
She is going back home, to Africa.
I feel left behind.

I put her clothes into the washing machine last night at 23.09.
And this morning at 6.33 I hung them on the line.
She was still lying in bed in my room.
It seemed like touching the clothes of a dead body.

But she is alive and she seems happy.
It is my heart that feels dead.
And my mind, even though at the same time
it is too aware, sensitive, lucid.
I feel the pain as a net of sharp heavy crystals falling on me.
It is surreal and slow and hurtful.
The distances, departures, farewells
enter, pierce, break through me.

8.06 am. I am in the office. I talk to the cleaning lady.
A young mother from Mauritius.
She talks about food, her Hindu food.
I ask her name and how to spell it.
I am about to say mine.
Carla, she says, *I know. I know your desk.*
I see your notes on your desk every morning, she says.

9.39 am. This is not the end. But feels like nothing else.

ANNIE DEPPE

 Annie Deppe was born in Hartford, Connecticut, in 1950, and is the author of *Sitting in the Sky*, a book of poems published by Summer Palace Press in 2003. A new collection entitled *The Wren's Cantata* appeared from Summer Palace Press in autumn 2009. Her work has been included in *The Forward Book of Poetry 2004*. She holds an MA in Creative Writing from Lancaster University in England and has taught poetry at Eastern Connecticut State University. She received a grant from the Irish Arts Council and was part of Poetry Ireland's Introduction Series in 2002. She has published on both sides of the Atlantic, including in Ireland *Poetry Ireland Review*, *The Stinging Fly*, *The SHOp*, and *The Recorder*. She holds an MA in Educational Psychology and Special Education from the University of Connecticut. A native New Englander, she now holds dual US-Irish citizenship due to the luck of having Irish grandparents. She assists in running the Stonecoast in Ireland MFA programme, facilitates writing workshops and conferences, and offers mentoring and editing services to writers. She makes her home within sight of the sea on the west coast of Ireland.

Salt Over the Shoulder

What comes back now are fast walks on Falcarragh's back strand,
the sand no longer firm beneath our feet, and plovers
chasing each other in and out of the rolling edge.
Long talks of how we must, one day, leave everything.

Evenings, that winter, we read Akhmatova's poems aloud
and the city of Saint Petersburg filled our sitting room.
And once, when we stepped outside, the stars were the stars of Russia
and we remembered a friend who somehow resembled her:

that proud head, at times wrapped in a turban
to show off her long, Modigliani neck. Two lives
lived with the same passion, but one with reckless speed.
Paper. Salt. Stars. When are the sands ever firm?

After Emergency Surgery

Cradled in rare blue light
        the island spreads out

below. I didn't think I'd be able
        to return this year,

but here is the house
        with its stone table

and the sudden pheasant
        with its surprising red crown

and the cows' black flanks
        shimmering

in early Irish summer.
        Sounds of children

swimming in South Harbour,
        and all the while

a smell of fresh cut hay
        mixing somehow with lavender.

Sometimes
        I think of the soul

as a winged visitor,
        wandering here, then out of view.

Who made the painting
        that hangs in the Louvre

just to the right of Giotto's
        "St. Francis and the Birds"?

In it an angel kneels,
        offers Mary a lily

as he rends
        her life.

Each word a miracle,
        but it's the riffs of plumage,

the rainbowed wings,
        that steal the show,

as if the painter
        could not restrain himself,

as if paradise
        were a tropical island

which he'd once
        caught sight of.

A farmer burns gorse
        at the end of the Bill,

black-backed gulls glide
        through the plumes

but just beyond this,
          against the background

of blue, a single sail
          fills with light.

I travelled that way myself
          this spring,

lay rocking in bed
          as my boat rose,

the vibrations of something
          I could not see

keeping me company
          throughout the night

though I remember
          no birds, or angels.

But there was something
          like a sail—

no paradise,
          not even a lily—

something, like
          the trembling of a sail.

The Glass Bell

Winter arrives early to this house above the sea.
November gales filled with sleet
blast the western windows, so as evening falls

mid-afternoon I wonder how the new red calf
will survive the night. Ten years ago
we sold the family home

and since I'm the only one who's never gone back
to see what the new owner's changed,
for me, the door latch still rattles

at the bottom of the stairs and the soft tick
of the mantel clock goes on as though I am tucked in
sick on the daybed in my father's study

with a glass bell left at my side.
In the field the calf romps by its mother,
staying close. Strange how the books I loved best

were all about children surviving alone:
in boxcars, in barns, in a burnt-out tree,
in the ruined rubble of war-torn Warsaw.

Now across Gweebarra Bay, last light
falls on the deserted village from whose strand
we once carried a rock across the Atlantic

to use as a door stop.
But that was yet another house.
The question of seas, of how that inner place

of feeling completely at home can be cleaved
clear through. When we sold our parents' house
we took turns choosing furniture and

keepsakes then let the rest of it go.
Betrayals like this can be explained,
but not to the girl who often refused

to clean her closet for fear of
hurting the feelings of what she'd throw out.
I miss the lilacs and white clapboards now,

my mother's maple desk,
even the sound of the bell
which once could call my mother to my side.

On the Lake Road Out of Maghery

After a phone call with our younger son
in which he described his home above Willow Creek
as an orchard by the sky,

I walk the lake road out of Maghery,
watch cygnets try their wings,
long feet skimming then lifting

from that radiance.
If I had to say where my heart dwells now,
one answer would be in pieces

with my far-flung family,
but another might be along this marshy stretch
of restless reeds and swans.

Neither firm land, nor water.

THEODORE DEPPE

Ted Deppe was born in the U.S. in 1950 and moved to Ireland in 2000. He is a dual citizen and now lives in County Galway. In the U.S., his work has been recognized by two fellowships from the National Endowment for the Arts and a Pushcart Prize. His books of poetry include *Orpheus on the Red Line* (Tupelo, 2009), *Cape Clear: New and Selected Poems* (Salmon, 2002), *The Wanderer King* (Alice James, 1996) and *Children of the Air* (Alice James, 1990). He worked as an RN for almost two decades and has taught in graduate programs in Ireland, England, and the U.S. He served as Writer in Residence at the James Merrill House in Stonington, Connecticut and at Phillips Academy in Andover, Massachusetts. He presently directs Stonecoast in Ireland, a programme that allows Master's students in the U.S. to study in Ireland.

The Singing

That morning, two nuthatches sauntered head-first down the pine
to a place where it was written in the wind *Yes, they like it,*

and for that moment it was the house of the world,
the green bough where they chatted and strolled upside-down.

Then, our daughter called from Greece,
giving her first and last name as if to make sure

we knew who she was. Her four-thousand-miles-away voice
pleaded for help as a man hammered on heavy glass

and we thought we'd have to listen to each scream of her rape,
or murder. No. Neighbours intervened. We stayed on the phone

until a woman told us, *Stop worry. Please, stop worry.*
Alone again in our living room my wife said she felt *weak*

from the inside out, and I asked if she'd heard
something like a girl chanting the whole time. *There was this*

singing on the line, I said, but my wife hadn't heard it
and answered, *Do I have to start worrying about you now?*

I've never mentioned it again, it must have been some part of
        myself,
some knowledge that we can't, finally, keep each other safe.

Our daughter changed her ticket, crossed the night, and came
        home,
though what home is keeps changing since that call.

There is a map and a clock and a humming in the room,
there is coffee, or champagne and kofta curry,

there is a family, or at least the hope that someone might, if not
rescue us, hear us. There is this chatting together

as we amble about upside-down and try to get used
to the perspective. And there is this shared time,

which is the green bough, for which I am grateful.

The Funeral March of Adolf Wölfli

*—From the oral history of Lisa Becker taken in Berne,
Switzerland, 1970.*

I found that art would keep him quiet. After breaking
a fellow patient's wrist, he was isolated for years

—I brought him colored pencils and newsprint
and he drew all day, or composed music in a system

God revealed to him. For a time he thought he loved me.
For a time my face appeared in every drawing he made.

He wrote the Santa Lisa Polka for me, hardly danceable, but—
despite the home-made paper trumpet he hummed on—

haunting, and mine. He said, once, if I married him,
he'd abdicate his kingdom, write a waltz for me each day.

Strange, then, after he died, to search in vain
through his eight-thousand-page Funeral March, looking

for something—anything—I could play before we buried him.
His masterpiece reached to the ceiling of his cell,

hand-sewn scores in which the music constantly gave way
to drawings or ads from magazines. What might have been

eighth notes floated above maps or rambling prayers,
and then staves appeared with no notes at all—

this was the work he'd curse me for disturbing!
The night before his funeral, I sorted through

those composition books and found no sustained melody—
but what did I expect? When he worked, he had a ritual

of rolling up his shirt sleeves and trousers
that took hours, interrupted by his voices. He'd start

drawing in the margins and press inward, filling each space,
singing to himself like a boy. Oh, he was more selfish

than a child, incapable of loving anyone. I never told him
I wasn't married. I took care of him thirty years, longer

than most marriages last! Such a strange, ugly fellow—
our yellow-fingered, warp-nailed, one-man Renaissance.

He'd consume his week's supply of pencils in three days,
then beg for more—against the doctor's orders I gave them.

His March was signed, "St. Adolf, Chief Music Director,
Painter, Writer, Inventor of 160 Highly Valuable Inventions,

Victor of Mammoth Battles, Giant-Theatre-Director,
Great God, Mental Patient, Casualty."

In some ways I was relieved when he died, as if a blizzard
finally howled away and I could start to shovel out.

He didn't want to leave a few perfect works behind him.
He wanted to lift up everything, wanted to give

the whole dying world lasting form.
There were lucid moments when he knew he was mad—

he could almost imagine what a normal life might be.
I'd go home and practice piano every night.

I'd play Beethoven, feel the moments things caught fire,
but couldn't myself become flame.

Page upon page of his March, containing, he said, everything
and everyone he'd ever loved, and not a single tune

I could play for his funeral. Not even the Santa Lisa Polka.
We buried him without music. There is nothing

I blame myself for more. We buried him without music
and for two weeks I took to bed. Then one night—

it was snowing—I rolled up the sleeves of my nightdress.
I pinned up the hem, then puzzled over a line of music

that vanished in a field of painted irises, purple flags
instead of notes waving under a sky of sharps and flats.

I closed my eyes and began to play. I didn't know
what my hands were doing. Snow kept falling,

silences tumbled forward, winged notes soared
above chipped ivory keys. I played what I could

of his Funeral March—imperfectly, of course,
only in fragments—I played the Funeral March

of Adolf Wölfli, everything dark, falling, silver.

Marisol

When I quit my nursing job
to write in Ireland,
I stepped out into summer stars

and clicked my heels in the air.
Security cameras
caught my leap

and the supervisor
froze the frame all night
so day shift could see
that look of pure joy.

Strange now, to think
Marisol had just been readmitted.

Did Dante feel guilty
as he left the inferno?—all those voices calling,
remember us to the living—

I can be watching the island children
run down the pier after a field trip
to the mainland, or a hooded crow
might crack a mollusk on the rocks, and—

Beautiful Marisol.
Her pale, dirty face framed
by matted black hair.

Some keenness behind those dark eyes
as if she'd been raised by wolves.
Marisol, who'd stabbed her foster father
with a pencil: her fourth failed placement.

Marisol, who'd first
come to our children's unit
when she was five—something broken
behind those eyes, and fierce—

At the seawall, the island children call
to the spring tide to swell up
and pelt them
with rocks and spray.

They shriek, cover their heads and run,
then return laughing to the slipway
and taunt the sea again.

And the children in the hospital courtyard?
Those who will call out to anyone
beyond the high, link fence?
Want to or not, I see them:

Marisol strides on low stilts
through the locked garden
and won't look at her birthmother

who's finally come to visit.
She plants one leg down and
swings her hip into the next step:

her mother and that nurse
can go to hell
till this dance is played out,

back straight, head high,
everyone calling.

Guillemot

Mother hadn't shied from the word *cancer*,
but I needed time to hear it, listened instead to the cries

of oystercatchers flying low across South Harbour.
With each wave's retreat, rocks tumbled down

the steep slope, grinding and knocking, making a falling
music to go with the sea's *hush*.

Then I saw the guillemots—shiny with oil
from some off-shore slick, they thrashed

in the small waves, flapping and toppling
in the push of stones. I might have rushed past, trying

not to look, but my friend arrived, we flung
our coats over two birds and bundled them home.

The tub water blackened. They nipped each other. They bit us
until we learned to hold them by the back of their heads.

Like abused children, taken from their homes,
they lashed out as we tried to help.

The guillemots aren't your mother, my wife said. I knew that,
but sliced wide-eyed herring, willing the birds to eat,

though only one did, making strange castanet sounds
with its black bill as it swallowed. When the smaller bird died

we set up a mirror in the cage and the survivor haunted it,
seeking a way back to the world of guillemots.

During the holidays, I helped dig a grave
for a German woman who'd loved this island—

as our coats swayed in lichened branches,
we loosened the ground with pick axes, took turns digging,

then cleaned our hands in the wet grass. Next day
we walked behind the rusted blue Volvo. Waves

exploded against the far cliffs, two island girls
played slow airs, and death seemed almost something kind.

Another phone call from the States: before her first round
of chemo, Mother went sledding with my brother's sons,

so which bird is not my mother, the one that died
or the one we released on Christmas Eve?

Today, a Christmas letter arrives
from a Chinese friend, who wishes for my wife:

*I hope Annie will enjoy to walk and tilt herself
in great wing but not worry about felling in that small*

and beautiful island. In the moments before sleep,
the line comes back in the dark like a prayer I need

to repeat for us all: let us enjoy to walk and tilt
in great wing. Let us not worry about the felling.

GABRIEL EZUTAH

 Gabriel Ezutah was born in Ohafia, Nigeria in 1965. His father told him numerous stories as a child, which helped lay the foundation for his creative career. His poetry has appeared in newspapers, poetry newsletters and anthologies in Nigeria, Ireland and the United States of America. Gabriel Ezutah moved to Ireland in 2001 and lives in Kinsale where he works in a hotel. His first book of poetry, *Pebbles of Sound,* was published in 2003. His first novel, *Trail of Immortality,* is in the process of being published in the United States of America. He is writing his second novel and has thousands of unpublished poems. Gabriel is a voracious reader, loves to run and swim, and considers himself a spiritual writer. He has several of his poems on his website: www.gabrielezutah.com and blogs on gabrielezutah.blogspot.com

The Tree of Love

Love hung from her low branches
like rich grapes in happy seasons
and she urged me to pluck at will.

She displayed her rose petals
without the hidden, snaring thorns.

She was as sweet as wild honey
without the nuisance of angry bees.

She dripped like perennial dew
on a lost friend in a baking desert.

I planted my love on a mountaintop
and used the meter of her cool shadow
to judge every cannibal spider.

Electric Fish

Freedom, in her simple and free ways
    is a puppy.
        Who dares to put a leash on the Wind?
        Who could tie Spirit to the stake?
Try diverting the wild ocean.

Freedom, in her plain and self-willed ways
    is an electric-fish.
        Love admires her waterway beauty with awe
            but grabbing hands harvest slime and air
and perhaps a few slaps and a rude shock.

LISA FRANK

 Lisa Frank was born in Los Angeles, California in 1970. After spending most of the past ten years living in the Pacific Northwest, she moved to Ireland in 2007. She received her MFA in Creative Writing from Eastern Washington University in 2005 and has had work published in a multitude of genres, including fiction, poetry, creative nonfiction and screenwriting, in both the US and Ireland. She has taught creative writing in a variety of settings, including an urban high school in Los Angeles, a medium-security mens' prison and a university in Washington state. She currently works as a freelance editor and is the editor for *Doire Press*, a small literary publisher in Connemara, where she lives with her partner.

Stain

Scrubbing the counter
in the bathroom, my cold chaffed hands
pushing the sponge
round and around, slowly
scraping away
the dried clots from the tile
as the sound of the ambulance
echoes through my head.
Will they get here fast enough?

I watched as they wheeled my father away
still in his faded blue pinstriped pajamas
and blood down the back of his head.

Later he reassures me it's just the medication.
'Sometimes it makes me dizzy,' he says.
But medication or no, he'll be dead
in four weeks' time.

I dip the sponge into the bucket
and watch the water slowly cloud red
seeing a flash of my father
at my bedroom door, hands gripped
to the doorframe, blood in a streak
down the side of his face.

I breathe deeply and rinse the sponge.
Then I start cleaning the counter
all over again.

3 November 2004

Walking down a mid-size street
in a mid-size city
in some strangled mid-size
American state
staring at the ground, the leaves
in a sludgy black mess of snow
underneath my feet.

The streets are empty, doors
closed tight.
No noise of children
or sound of birds
voices muted, too numb to speak.

The Pacific breeze blows
crisp on my face. But today
it's not enough—
the air is just too thick
to breathe.

When I reach my door
I look up at the sky and wonder
how to say sorry
to the rest of the world
for four more years.

MATTHEW GEDEN

 Matthew Geden was born in the English Midlands in 1965, growing up in Coventry and moving to Kinsale, Co. Cork in 1990. Since then he has had poems published in numerous magazines, journals and anthologies throughout Ireland and abroad. Some of his poems have been translated into Croatian and Gallician. He has also translated a number of poems into English including work by Apollinaire, Montale and Catullus. He was educated at University College Cork and now runs an independent bookshop in Kinsale. In recent years Geden has also organised talks, readings and co-founded both SoundEye Festival of the Arts of the Word and Engage: Bandon Arts Festival. His publications include several chapbooks such as *Kinsale Poems* and *Autumn: Twenty Poems by Guillaume Apollinaire,* both published by Lapwing. A first full-length collection, *Swimming to Albania,* was published by Bradshaw Books in 2009.

Photosynthesis

How plant-like we've become.
Your finger fronds limp from days of rain
curl around the steering-wheel. A low
pressure rests on our shoulders, the tension
of being kept in the dark too long. We
sway like half-drunk poppies. The car lurches

through stony silence. At the shore
we stop in the grey mist, your lips the only
colour for miles. Yet suddenly there is
a glimmer. The gloom recedes and figures

come out of the haze. The sea becomes
a white-haired Turner throwing light upon

our predicament. Even my predilection for
definition is surprised by the sudden edge
and the realisation that everything we see
is luminance. Out of the car I straighten up.
Reaching for warmth I part the clouds,
soak up sunlight and begin to breathe

more easily. You are there beside me.
We breathe together noticing shades and
textures as if for the first time.
Your eyes are many colours. Re-energised
we share complexities. We nourish each
other and scatter our hopes to the wind.

To A Friend

After Mugan, d. 1374

Suddenly the old farmer called us back
To drink three pints in the evening light.
Humanity is small but this drunkenness vast and marvellous—
Where now is England, where your empire?

JOHN GIVENS

 John Givens was born in Northern California in 1943. He got his BA in English literature at the California State University Fresno and his MFA in creative writing at the Iowa Writers' Workshop, University of Iowa, where he was a Teaching/Writing Fellow. He was a U.S. Peace Corps Volunteer in South Korea for two years; he studied language and art in Kyoto for four years; and he worked as a writer and editor in Tokyo for eight years. For fifteen years, Givens worked as a creative director and branding consultant for advertising agencies in New York and San Francisco. He has published three novels in the US: *Sons of the Pioneers, A Friend in the Police,* and *Living Alone*; short stories have appeared in various journals. His non-fiction publications include *A Guide to Dublin Bay: Mirror to the City* and *Irish Walled Towns,* both published by The Liffey Press in Dublin. He is currently finishing a long novel set in seventeenth-century Japan. "Eastern Howth Sequence" is a modern adaptation of the traditional Japanese form, haikai linked poetry.

Eastern Howth Sequence

1.
Gorse blooms then heather;
Irish Sea clouds slide over
lichens on limestone.

2.
Gray summer showers:
auks quicker than kittiwakes
under the cliff walk.

3.
Slopes rusting bracken;
cormorants, gannets and terns:
each flies its own way.

4.
Autumn drizzle all day;
on the shell of a big snail
rides a smaller one.

5.
Winter seclusion:
peat briquettes for two weeks,
whiskey for half that.

6.
Foghorns in snowfall;
a seagull glides out of whiteness
and back into it.

7.
Things just as they are:
the ordinary sun rises
again and again.

PAUL GRATTAN

 Paul Grattan was born in Glasgow in 1971. He moved to the North of Ireland in 1995 to study an MA in Creative Writing under the late James Simmons at the Poet's House, Portmuck, Co. Antrim. He lived in Dublin for seven years teaching English as a Foreign Language and Creative Writing before returning to Belfast in 2005. He is currently researching the work of the Scottish Poet and Cultural thinker Kenneth White for a PhD at the Academy of Irish Cultural Heritages, University of Ulster. His first collection of poems, *The End of Napoleon's Nose*, was published by the Edinburgh Review in 2002 and his work has appeared in many journals and anthologies. He lives, for his sins, in Belfast.

Daytime Astronomy

after Pollock

In which a young man lies on his back
staring up at the sky. He seems to be home
but some of the trees are kin and rimed
with ice while others are in full leaf.

There are flowers in the grass
but they are horrible, pustular excrescences
and the loan all wrong. Perhaps
he has more portentous limits

in mind. Outflows of rock porridge,
starry pins and sacrificial beams, a bone
skull, its ritual markings mulched

by millet. Little by little he is transformed
or stilled or occupied by grass lying
outside his barn painting or hypnotized
by the Hamptons or momentarily halted,
bounded by this solitude of stone.

An Act of Completion

> *So then because thou art lukewarm,*
> *and neither cold nor hot, I will spew thee*
> *out of my mouth*
> —Rev. 3:16

I thought at Lurgan I had found my European home.
Yet how little people care for the tenderness of page,
all those good or bad intentions with which
ordinary looks are paved and how much we sink

in those few fields submerged a mile or so outside
a lion's den from which no tracks return. Mad Pup
lies wounded boss, not dead but does any of it hold water?
A rictus of the hood whose fink is loyalty, that blue

nun of the damned. What has mythology to do
with being wrong? In the mirror let it be read,
Da' built his pecs like Oppenheimer built his bomb—at night,
in kinky black and white, for want of devastation.

Mad bitches on the platform slink to polished chrome
by so much vaunted, damp and massive hardness.
These are my daughters and my daughters' days,
blink and be born again beyond completion.

Sick Child, Bed City

"Ut pictura, poesis"—Horace

Scittery, scattery do you lie, after a winter's teat,
in neat American Freedom baby-grow, our baby Lenin
lookey-likey. To make words love, love, under the arbour
that hangs on the hill, *Mons Palatinus*, Sorrento's chip,
rent town of crane and Cappuccino. All touching
pressure given with lips, formed by the breath,
uttered by mouth, held by the ear, set down by fingers,
swell to the eye you inhabit more than one wing,
peasant scenes and faces, canvases creatured
by Turner's seascapes, interiors and visions,

paint puffs Horace never knew. Teething on raw
enchantment, you are the spit of Metsu's sick child,
forcefully drawn, listlessly tender, an untouched
earthenware bowl of pap, bare beside a brownish ankle.

Carvery Country

What makes this country free
is the butterflies plamossing
the vestiges of a breeze

at some stop that's not for changing
of the gauges, herald-mothing
the heartland. I will never sit

comfortably with the Fianna
removed from this village life
mutt and jeff to my people's song

a shift in skies that makes me
brilliantly upset. Too aloof
for translation, I'll be an under-

stander, midget-wrangler, curly-
bap-straightner, or the sign reading
you have now left Carvery Country.

SHANE GUTHRIE

 Shane Guthrie was born in Seattle, WA, USA in 1978. He has been writing poetry since 1993, when he discovered it was a better outlet for his emotions than playing football. Having completed a degree in Computer Science from Western Washington University, he went to work shortly after for a large multinational corporation. This job allowed him to transfer to Dublin, with his wife Rebecca Diamant Guthrie.

'When I was in elementary school'

When I was in elementary school
First grade, perhaps
One day the teacher gave us
A Dixie cup
Two spoonfuls of dirt
And a single seed

We dutifully wrote our names on the cups
Pushed the seed into the dirt
And set them in the window
We overwatered them
They sprouted
And over spring break
Died
Shriveled down to stringy, emaciated ghosts

I don't know what
The lesson was supposed to be
But what I learned
Is that life is very, very fragile

'And Socrates lost an ear'

And Socrates lost an ear
When the bust hit the marble floor
With a great crack
In the silence of the museum

Docents came running
Like it was Murder
And I put my hands up
Not sure what they'd do

But they rushed to the broken ear
Sending everyone away
While I apologized and apologized

Two weeks later
You couldn't tell the difference
Sometimes I think the artifacts
Are mostly glue

MIRELA NICOLETA HINCIANU

 Mirela Nicoleta Hincianu was born on the 2nd of December 1978 in Galati, Romania, a town on the banks of the Danube where she grew up and was later employed as a social worker for three years, supporting and working with troubled and disabled young people. Four years ago she chose Ireland as her adoptive home and began to write two years after arriving here. In 2008, she published her first piece of writing, an essay which was included in a book published in Romania, as well as a collection of essays and poems. She is currently working on two other volumes and is collaborating on a number of Romanian literary websites.

Irish Paths

Astray on Irish paths
I whistle a tune of homesickness,
root about in smells,
in chestnut blossoms.

Darkness dies
in the eye of a mirror.
It was a square of happiness
that broke apart into sins,
seven in number like the years.
I feel the greenness of trees,
the cube-shaped piece in the cup of life,
coffee tasting of morning.

What remains are the sediments of feelings
punctured in the shape of a shoe sole.

Search for the steps of time inside me

The Moon Divided Into You, Into I

At night the moon descended towards
the diaphanous folds of the window
there was such air between us
we shared one breathing
but the moon was a ling torn in two
and from the leftovers
I fed the angels
with pearls of rain,
of wind, of storm.

we were away
inside ourselves
watched through the streak of darkness
as the moon divided
into you
into I

JOSEPH HORGAN

 Joseph Horgan was born in Birmingham, England in 1964 to a mother from Cork and a father from Kerry. He has lived in Ireland since 1999. His poems have been published in various magazines and in 2003 he was shortlisted for the Hennessy Award for New Irish Writing. In 2004 he was the winner of the Patrick Kavanagh Award. *Slipping Letters Beneath the Sea,* from which these poems are taken, is his first collection and was published by Doghouse in 2008. His work has been broadcast on RTÉ radio and television. He writes a weekly column for *The Irish Post.*

Like Skin

My father is eighty-eight years old.
An often silent man
from a generation of silent men
that emigrated with suitcases wrapped in string
to lie awake in another country,
staring at their lives through the ceiling,
remembering cold water and a Christmas cupboard
that held exotic fruit; oranges and bananas.
Fruit corrupts, grows parched like paper, like skin.

Placing bets, buying drinks, staring at the ceiling,
in the lee of his silent life I am walking.

Minor Movements in the History of Emigration

i
We come from
the little monasteries,
small farms,
damp houses.

ii
I leave knowing
that I will only ever be
of this parish.

The sea mocks me,
childhood voices taunt me.
I have left.

iii
We leave no love behind
in that country of the white ditches.
Night, day and half-day,
the company of men.
Bare stones in a field.

Telegrams

For immigrants
death came mainly in the post.
A respectful knock on the door.
A letter slipped beneath the sea.

The telegrams would bring to mind
the tele-printer.
Uncle Dead Stop
Blues 6 Villa 2 Stop.

Mostly bodies we didn't know,
vague names,
sketched outlines in life,
corporeal now in death.

But for you
the death was an accusation,
carelessly flung,
the final ripples of your estrangement.

Imperial Road

i

There was no river in my youth,
no horse thief or chicken-killing fox
but in our city backyard
my father and I would sit
at the lapping edge of a sea.

ii

Immigrants lose their minds in crossing,
misplace them behind the draughty door
of the damp place they leave.
When belongings are eventually sent on
they are never unpacked
for fear of what is broken.

iii

My father studied horses and hunches.
My mother came ashore again below white clouds,
trailing curled hair and a childhood
and she often halted there, where the train was waiting.

ORITSEGBEMI EMMANUEL JAKPA

 Oritsegbemi Emmanuel Jakpa lives in Ireland. His poetry has been published in a number of online and print journals including *African American Review,* and *Echoing Years: an Anthology of Poetry from Canada and Ireland.* He is a Yeats' Pierce Loughran Scholar.

Birthday Party

1

Victor says he is always indoors
& does not go out to the night club
because a nightclub bouncer
told him that he is not welcome there.

Then Michael tells him
that if he knows his rights
no one will do that to him.
Segun, leaning lazily to one side of his chair,
shouts that Victor did the right thing.

Now they mute their voices,
as I am about to speak, as if my words
sag with weight & blaze with importance.
"Victor are you sure,"
I ask. He says, yes.

2

Now they start to talk
the way all angry
people do.

I intrude again & ask him what really happened.
Words like these are hard to swallow.
Again, they keep quiet
as he disengages his voice
from the hoarfrost & icicles of their silence
to speak as if it was all planned.

He says he was drinking his Guinness,
sitting, still looking out,
for a girl to dance with,
when the bouncer came & told him
that he his not welcome there.

3

Now their voices rise
on steam wings of their passions,
spill into each other,
not to & fro, but up and down
on pedals of emotions.
They are talking all the time
half eating, half drinking,
in different tones
& gestures of annoyance.

But see how beautiful they look
spooning their rice

& guzzling their beer.
But see how beautiful this argument takes them whole
into its mouth.

Harmattan

after Seamus Heaney

Outside my window
the digger, digging,
plunges the spade into gravelly ground
that hisses needle-edge-sharp sound
into palpable rhythm
as green buds crack in the dry harmattan,
throws dust around.

The land trenches longer & deeper
by each successive glint
of the spade.

During its aerial suspension,
he pauses, stares into blue haze
that mirages over on the noon highway,
and thinks of the years he spent
in Kirikiri prison, useless
as free papers
in a printing press;

of his friends who disappear like methylated spirit
and his father's tutelage: firewood
is only for those who can take heart,
that is why not all can gather it.

He shakes his head.
Grip, grip, grip hard
& downright down strikes
the vengeful spade.

2.

In our airtight dragnet, roadblocks everywhere.
Borders tight as steel ziplocks
checkmate every hope.
Yet many people of lesser talent
slip out, unabated, with ease.

The logic of existence
replants us in alien soil.
We tear round the hairpin
corners of the word, divided to the vein:
to stay put or to go.

So, the periodic spade strikes, each stroke
the rasped desolation and anger of the soul.
Tribulations of a black-gold age.
The excavations and makings
of our blood, and drainage.

Before the harmattan and the digger
unmoving I sit;
before their intimate vengeance
a watcher.

My pen, my spade.
I'll crack with it.
Dig with it.

Connemara

for Joan McBreen

whatever ink I use to write
Tullycross
whatever lens I choose

to capture Connemara
whatever spot I lay down my grief
or pick up joy

whatever Audigier
in her backyard garden paints
with hurricanes

from hair driers
whatever river coils among these hills
over a land of silence

and distance
this place fills me with the honey
of untouched time

PAUL JEFFCUTT

 Paul Jeffcutt was born in a hamlet near the border between England and Wales. He has lived and worked in three different continents and has travelled widely; he's settled amidst drumlins in the peaceful green countryside of County Down. His poems have appeared in poetry journals across Europe, Australia and the USA, including *Stylus, Crannóg, Grapevine, Mobius, Revival* and *Silkworm;* his poems have also featured in anthologies from established poetry presses including Ragged Raven Press, Biscuit Publishing, Currock Press and Cinnamon Press. In 2006, he read in the Poetry Ireland Introductions Programme. His poetry has been broadcast by BBC Radio Ulster. He has also read his work at venues across the island, including the Irish Writers' Centre and Damer Hall (in Dublin), at the Belfast Festival and the Between the Lines Festival (in Belfast) and at the Market Place Theatre (in Armagh). He was selected to read at the first Poetry Circuit of Ireland, organised in Belfast by the NI Creative Writer's Network. He is a longstanding member of the Writers' Group at the Seamus Heaney Centre for Poetry in Belfast.

English at Nightschool

Ernesto's stubble matches the black leather—
the jacket crinkles
but his face doesn't.
Playing teacher, I beam and joke;
he grips the book like a shield,
staring into it
uncomprehending
and resentful.

Flood

It lashes the shipyard city -
sousing inky slates, rills squirt,
torrents plunge into gutter seas;
leaky boots, I'm scuppered
on the long slosh home.

Good Friday's spring tide
ebbs, sweet-wrappers frothing;
darkened taxi snouts the waves
to shabby pool of tinkling light -
another for the road?
Dispatched down a laneway,
sodden memorial blooms
lie spent and wasting.

A periscope scans refugee streets,
convoys of terraces holed in action;
illustrated gables shudder
and groan, going down,
all dogs baying.

ENRIQUE JUNCOSA

 Enríque Juncosa (born in Palma de Mallorca, Spain, 1961) has published six collections of poetry. The last two will be published in English in 2010 in a single volume, *Bay of Flags and Other Poems,* by the Dedalus Press, translated by Michael Smith, who also translated the two poems which follow here. Juncosa is also the director of the Irish Museum of Modern Art since 2003, where he edits the magazine *Boulevard Magenta.* Before that he was deputy director of the Museo Nacional Centro de Arte Reina Sofía in Madrid. Juncosa has curated shows of many artists including Dorothy Cross, Howard Hodgkin, Miroslaw Balka, James Coleman or Terry Winters.

The Secret Life of Poets

Lizards and ocelots in a grove
of bamboo
lately drenched by the rain.

Also red flowers, dragonflies
and blue birds.

Clouds bestow on the world a grey and humid tone
and the sun scarcely appears
gently chapping
the tall tops of the trees.

I am searching for this chink in myself,
surrounded by pagodas,
while the tropical storm rages.

Frogs are unceasing marimbas
syncopating with precision
above my breathing.
Dark lakes are transformed by the light
into liquid crystals ...
perhaps untenable legends.

Emerald and black lights
in starred and deep spaces
where hummingbirds are lyrical raptures.

Cascades
          of petals
                    of fire.

The depth of kisses is a perfect
song
and whispering voices water
transformed into steam
as they brush against skin and tongue.

Angels exist and they're us
eyes of uranium,
triceps of chrome,
pagan deities ...

In girum imus nocte et consumimur igni.

Dragonflies and Gamelan

for Catherine Lampert

Dragonflies
hypnotised
by their own reflection
in the still water
of a Malayan novel.

Glass Javanese
beads
and the fabric of the soul
of the Batak in Sumatra.

Marionettes and metallic
drums,
music of gold,
erratic but concentric
butterflies:

Borobudor:
Coconut palms, zebus and palaces.

These lotus flowers
further beyond winter
and the world of rain.

To live here
as in the pages of books
never to return.

El Capricho

for Victor Esposito

The days are blue
and dry
and a muscular wind
        veils and unveils them
           with swift white linens.

The house is hidden
           among the poplars
that, besides, arrange
           violet fields of alfalfa
along a line of willows
           sketched by a river
              of translucent,
             silvery
               and frozen water.

I walk beneath the willows
           raising
             ibises
that honk
      their horns
           as if they were a flute.

The willows end
and the river winds
in sandy regions
      and terraces
           of boulders.
Dogs race after
      jumping hares

dodging bushes
and several black vultures
    are picking at the bones
        of what was a goat.

Behind the wires
that limit *El Capricho*
an arid steppe
of beetles appears
forming rounded hills
flecked with hawthorns
and shrubs.

The hares continue on
        like capricious projectiles
            alerted by pairs of gendarmes:
Lapwings
    are telltale
        and noisy birds.

Once at the summit of the hill
I contemplate
again
the poplar groves
and the willows that form an oasis
        in the vastness of the steppe
            under the snowcapped peaks
of the Andes.

A flock of guanacos
    takes fright.
        They leap
            like antelopes
                raising

fine

dust clouds.

My skin burns
in the southern sun.

Clouds move
        so that it seems it's the earth
                        that moves,
and my breathing is a province of the wind
plunged in rebellion.

There is no one.
Only scattered livestock
and the smell of dry earth.

Here everything is beauty, everything order

Everything luxury and peace, our delight.

I have just read the last volume
of Sándor Márai's diaries
in which he describes his wife's death,
his companion of sixty years
before taking his own life.
It is a hard and lapidary book
like this landscape
in which it also arose:
her voice smelled of flowers.

Shrubs of tiny flowers

surround me,
precisely:
stonecrops and orchids,
both yellow,
also pink and white
thyme,
fuchsia stalks,
little peaches and fiery
red shrubs,
ochre and orange
verbum
and other flowers with names
I still don't know.

The thorny garden
natural
to the steppe
    like a coded plan
        of one's burning memory.

Faraway
    I hear horses
        neighing.

MATT KIRKHAM

 Matt Kirkham was born in Luton, England in 1966. He lives in Co. Down's Ards peninsula where he is a member of the Write!Down writers' collective. His debut collection *The Lost Museums* (Lagan Press, 2006) won the Rupert and Eithne Strong prize for first collections in Ireland. Matt's work was been anthologised in *Poetry Introductions* (Lagan Press, 2004), *Incertus* (Netherlea, 2007), *Our Shared Japan* (Dedalus, 2007) and *The New North* (Wake Forest University Press, 2008).

The Museum of Chillies

I'm waiting, in my Skoda,
for the lights to turn.
It's no news that history

can make men cry. The tarmac here is scorched
where boys set a bus burning
like the mouth of a conquistador.

Ovid's First Haibun

Before the hybrid Lexus of the Emperor's agent had reached the
bend in the country road I had set my laptop on the table by the
cottage window and my carved wooden horse by the laptop,
looking over the letter Q. Should I need to describe it in
translation to one of the poets of the East where they see our
alphabet as something raw or ill-refined, something lifted from
nature, from its basic shapes, I would set out for Q an image of an

old pond and the path of a frog's leap into it before we hear the ripples. It is the grey heron's eye and her beak that pierces the pond's meniscus and plucks up the frog. It is the inland sea and the flight of the heron towards it, drawn by the tides and the habits of the small fry. It is the wheel and the exhaust of the Lexus on a peninsula road charged with mayblossom and on the steering wheel the hand and wrist of the Emperor's agent tasked with driving the poet here into exile and with telling him that the book that obsesses the people here could either be the lexicon of its unique geography or an atlas of its strange dialect. Neither poet nor agent look up to see the heron flying above them. It is the thumb and forefinger of the Emperor's Chief of Police as he passes the agent a pen drive with a list of poets to be exiled and their offending lines, and it is the ring on the Emperor's ringfinger, the ring he turns and turns as he tries to remember lines from the poems the Chief of Police told him, the one about the family as cursed as the Emperor's own, the Emperor of another empire who raped his wife's sister and ate his own son stewed by his mother, those that turn at the prayer of the women from the rooftops and the forests into nightingale, swallow, hoopoe, and the one about the old pond and the frog.

> still as she can be
> heron marks the mother shore
> looking for movement

Poem to be Read in a Submarine

Everything, everyone
starts with a submarine.
The way a voice is wrapped
inside a phone this begins

as charged air wrapped in the sacks
of your lungs wrapped in flesh
wrapped in charged air wrapped in steel
and its buoyancy wrapped
in water-wrapped salt. Look back
down the long periscope
at the eye of Jules Verne,
a gap-toothed storyteller
in his grinning turban wrapped
in the Thousand and One Nights,
the way at this time of year
a mild shower is wrapped
in the sunlight of a week
of showers wrapped in sunlight.
It's been adrift in the lough
for months, him wrapped in the warmth
of his submarine wrapped
in undersea currents
but now Jules' sub is beached
at low tide. He opens
the hatch, crawls out in search
of seabirds, waders, the way
they overturn language
on the exposed mudflats.
In his belly a dunlin
sits wrapped in a sandwich tern
wrapped in a black-headed gull
wrapped in an oystercatcher
wrapped in a widgeon — you know,
you understand, you are wrapped
in the idea of being
wrapped in the idea as if
you inhabited the lungs
of a naked swimmer

who finds each of her hairs wrapped
in salt water. But the feast—
widgeon wrapped in a curlew
wrapped in a grey heron
wrapped in a Brent goose wrapped
in a cormorant. Jules' boat
floats and dives and drifts away
without him. From the shore
he watches its propellers
turn in the tides, light the towns
and when he opens his mouth
it's to free a parliament
of birds brushing the surface
of the lough as one bird.
A child points with one hand
while the other stays wrapped
around her toy submarine.

Song

After a mad show of a beating of wings
his beak releases its grip on her neck.
The air is flat. A curlew almost sings

of how some beasts take time over such things.
Of when I flicked the switch in last night's shed
and after a mad show of a beating of wings

the housemartin fledgling perched on my finger
a minute, two, of my time, before she flicked
into curved, bruised air. The curlew almost sings

and the roosters, the would-be kings,
Faverolle, Jersey Giant, crow and peck—
after a mad show of a beating of wings—

through the wire. Each summer morning brings
more notes in your song. I'll come back to bed.
The air is sweet. A curlew almost sings

that a song can rise from plucked strings
but all the words I've written and I've said
are a mad show of a beating of wings.
Air is musical. A curlew almost sings.

The Museum of the Colourblind

> *The great chemist John Dalton... had provided a classic
> description of red-green colourblindness in himself... and, indeed,
> willed an eye to posterity... Dalton's eye still resides, pickled, on a
> shelf in Cambridge.*
> —Oliver Sachs, An Anthropologist On Mars.

The testimony of John Dalton's eye:

Becalmed, soberly jarred, at the still eye
of no storm, high-
shelved with not a thing to eyeball, denied
even shut-eye, I visualise
a mosaic lobby floor. In my mind's
unreliable eye I glide
over green-red and red-green tesserae.
All I make out is The Use Of Colour.

With hi-fi eyesight you look me in the eye:
in those floor tiles you read *The Museum Of The Colourblind.*
Still, should I,
dyschromotope, give you the evil eye,
or, offered colour, answer *aye*
you'd see me lose what makes me I and I.

Painting rainbows I can't describe,
"Patch" Dalton flies straight through the needle's eye.
Bedazzled? Not I.

CHUCK KRUGER

Chuck Kruger was born 1938 in the USA and in 1966, along with his wife Nell, moved to Switzerland in protest against the Vietnam War, working as a literature teacher in an international school. In 1986 they purchased a farm on Clear Island, Co. Cork, where they moved permanently in 1992. Then he turned writer, poet, broadcaster and founded the Cape Clear International Storytelling Festival. He's won the Bryan MacMahon Short Story Competition 2003 (part of the Listowel's Writers' Week Festival), *The Dubliner* Short Story Contest 2002, the "How do I love thee?" 2004 Poetry Competition (UK), the Shinrone Poetry Festival 2002, and the *Cork Literary Review's* 2000 & 1998 Short Story Competitions. He has published 5 books to date: *Cape Clear Island Magic* (a collection of poems, short stories, essays, & photos) in 1994, reissued 1995 & 1999 & 2008 (an updated & expanded edition); an international thriller *The Man Who Talks to Himself* in 1998; two collections of short stories, *Flotsam & Jetsam* in 2000 and *Between a Rock* in 2005; and *Sourcing*, his first poetry collection, in 2008. For reviews and excerpts from his work, see www.chuckkruger.net

Digging

Turning village corner, I happen upon a harbour:
fifty craft at anchor—punts, dinghies, yachts;
half a dozen trawlers snug against the pier,
two old souls rotting in each others' arms,
all faintly familiar in the solstice dusk,
though I've never been in Skerries before.
As I stroll to the head of the L-shaped pier,

I spot three seals cavorting, slowly figure out
why they've gathered: aboard a blue trawler,
the *Ard-Mhuire*, five men work the port side,
five teenage boys the starboard,
while a lone lad shovels clear a path between.

I watch him push into a pulsing ton of pink
heaped mid-ship and heave prawn
onto tables either side. His colleagues sort,
kibitz, and when they toss something not so squirmy
overboard, the seals playfully submerge.

Half an hour later, I'm still watching from the dark
as the lad plows through the pile of flood-lit prawn.

The heap becomes a drift of snow
from my youth that's just slid off the roof
of my parents' upstate New York home and blocks
the drive. As the lad pushes in the shovel, steps
hard, stomps, flings another hundred prawn
onto table, I'm clearing my parents' drive
so dad can go to work tomorrow.

I wonder if I'll ever finish digging—
and as I leave the pier, I snack upon my memory
the way the seals chow down the throwaways.

Sister Skellig

Now I know why the monks did it,
hunkering down on that God
-unforsaken outpost of an Atlantic isle.

They didn't simply keep
turning the other cheek
alive.
In howling wind I hear them sing,
we're all we've got so on we go.

Now a beehive hut in a butterfly world
perched on the edge
of heritage
tells blow-in me not mainly of hardship
but of a wildly simplifying place, gull eggs,
pollack feathered from jagged ledge,
warmth the others in the hut,
a day-time look-out & blessed boulders
ready heavens above the single narrow path.
In howling wind I hear them sing,
we're all we've got so on we go.

Here on Cape, here on this sister isle,
in a practically unrelated time,
this is the way it should be:
Force 12 & the roof poised & so what,
mail delivered straight
to the living room table when we're not home,
keys left in car, a sea pink
swaying in a child's eagle eye,
intimacy with rambunctious Mother Nature
as existential as full flame
under fish-filled frying pan.
When I need help, or a neighbour mine,
that's it, off we go,
straight as the evening flight of a hooded crow.
In howling wind I hear them sing,
we're all we've got so on we go.

ANATOLY KUDRYAVITSKY

Anatoly (Anthony) Kudryavitsky was born in 1954 in Moscow of a Polish father and half-Irish mother. Educated at Moscow Medical University, he later studied Irish history and cultural heritage. Having lived in Russia and Germany, he now lives in Dublin and edits Shamrock Haiku Journal (www.shamrockhaiku.webs.com). His novel *The Case-Book of Inspector Mylls* was published by Zakharov Books (Moscow) in 2008. He also published a novella, a number of short stories and seven collections of his Russian poems. In 2005, Goldsmith Press published his first collection of English poems entitled *Shadow of Time*. His second collection, a book of his English-language haiku entitled *Morning at Mount Ring* (Doghouse Books), appeared in 2007. He has also published an anthology of contemporary Russian poetry in English translation entitled *A Night in the Nabokov Hotel* (Dedalus, 2006). His poems have appeared in magazines nationally and internationally and have been translated into eleven languages. He was the recipient of a number of literary awards, including Capoliveri Premio Internazionale di Poesia (Italy) and the Suruga Baika Prize of Excellence (Japan).

Lessons of Irregular History

Second World War began in 1933,
Hiroshima and Chernobyl in 1939;
papers do not report
if something's beginning today.

Lack of knowledge is reassuring.

In the garden of amnesia

raindrops land upon my radio
as it tells me in a hoarse voice
about people killed by fires
and frontier incidents.
However it doesn't hint that something's
beginning today.

I tune in the radio.
Now we hear the music of Mahler,
'St. Anthony of Padua Sermonising to Fishes'.
That music has no knowledge of today,
it narrates what has been going on
from the very sources of Irregular History,
while ill weeds form ears
and exceptions to Darwin's theory appear
in shady alleys.

Europe in the Mirror of my Teapot

is hard to recognize: this silvery curve
enlarges France and Germany
but lessens other states

Ireland is barely visible
Russia tends to slide away
to the dark side of existence

all the gaps between capes and islands
are mended
as if an invisible giant put in stitches

Croatia reaches for Italy
Sweden clings to Denmark

former mortal enemies give each other
hugs of love
maybe it was like that
in prehistoric times

this teapot seems to have its own vision
of the world
and the map of Europe on the wall

practically speaking
teapots serve another purpose
sipping my Bewleys tea

I wonder if I can see the meaning
in this image of unity and distortion
and also their strange synchrony

Out of Harm's Way

i.m. Daniel Harms, the Russian absurdist writer

Motorists own imaginary and non-existent things,
such as distances and remote countries.
Stepping on the accelerator,
they hasten the pace of a clock;
however time has to wait for slumbrous planes
pausing in the clouds.

Pedestrians own meadows and riverbanks.
Dawn and twilight mix colours for them;
the whole horizon encircles their eyeballs.

This autumn I, again, travel with strangers,
because only strangers travel.
Here, amidst the monotony of a German town
I am not familiar with,
time splits into grains of memory,
and I plunge into the quicksands of déjà vu.
It seems to me that I am walking along the street
from quite another German town.
The day has hidden its colours,
frames of a static theatre mist up,
and everything fades into grey,
comes to a halt.
Madness is never far away…

The next thing I see is a signboard:
'HARMS. TELEPHONE NUMBER 92 27 11'.
I begin to ponder that there's the multitude
of towns and countries,
the world is plagued with absurdity,
and there isn't many signboards like this!

Then the roaring of a motor pushes slightly
the frozen minute-hand.

Teddy Bear and a Russian Toy

'I may look softie but I have good principles,'
a Teddy bear growled.
'My maker once implied that he had put
a spring into my body,
the type that would never let me break down.
It appears that he was in earnest.

My eyes grow dim with each passing year,
my neck stiffens up, my ears are jammed
with the silly things I hear,
but my spring never fails to squeak.
What about you—
have you got a squeaky thing inside?'

Van'ka-Vstan'ka tilting doll rattled:
'My dear chap, look at me,
I am content with my lot.
Whatever happens, I never squeak,
and I am sure I don't need any spring.
You see, my centre of gravity is located
well below my belt.
If I get pushed, I'll straighten up with a playful smile,
no matter, rain or shine, wet or fine,
good times or bad times.'

'Now tell me the secret,
you phallic keeper of verticality,
you tireless Russky burden-bearer,'
the Teddy Bear snarled.
'Tell me, are they real, your blue eyes,
baby face and crimson blush?'

'No, they are limned,' the Russian toy tilted.
'But look at this paint—
    it doesn't peel, you know.'

SLAVEK KWI

Slavek Kwi is a sound-artist and composer fascinated by sound-environments. Interested also in free-music research as part of social investigation and employing the space and any objects it contains as musical instruments. His works oscillates between purely sound based and multidisciplinary projects. From the early nineties Slavek has operated under the name Artificial Memory Trace. Slavek Kwi was born in 1963 in former Czechoslovakia, lived for 14 years in Belgium and since 2000 has been based in Ireland. For details see www.artificialmemorytrace.com

(Untitled)

Memories are grassssssssshoppers.
Jump_pink bubbles of heat_ink splashed across my eyes
When I saw first time yourrrrr_red face
Laughing
Smiling
Not at me, but whole universe
Except me, ignoring me, not seeing me …
… how painful feeling stayed within my heart—imprinted on
cover of old suitcase, battered by travel in time … cornered fear
from my extinction as kind …
… such kind creature—giving away gifts of love!
Fortunate sur-faces-emerged in mirror
of grey-days-daisies sprinkled on canvas of grass.
Grassssssshoppers singing happy songs to my ears, hearing you
speak …
In exactly the same tone I remembered, when grasshoppers became
memories of happy childhood somewhere lost for ever in between

mountains like mist—eerie howls hovering in clouds of dew
suspended still—in stillness—between molecules of hot air
balloons—red—fear to fall—the edge of abyss—calling you ...
calling you ...
Put your hands on me,
... verify: I am The one!
The one belonging on miracle-side of love at first sight.
(And still not knowing)
Future is now,
Anytime I am true to myself
And to yooooooou, my love!
I love you.
Repeating like sacred mantra
In hope to stay—for—everrrrrr
Patterns of laughs,
As snails drooling their paths,
petals of forget-me-not dropping on the way
The way you first saw first blueberry
squashed red drop of sweet-ness-nest-s
Happiness, ...
Reminded, ...
Every-time ... experience-d.
To remmemmmber.
To not forget!
About love.
Never.
Forget not-e me. Not!
I am you.
As you see me.
And you are I, as I am Me.
Through our eyes, realize, how similar we are
stripped of image we imagine, we tell to each other, how we
imagine—how we are and forgetting act—now—as new blueberry
feeling sweet—simply. Every time you encounter me in your

world, as I am and as you are, rrrrrreally.
Yourrrrs.
Shadowsssssssssssssssss.

PAUL MADDERN

Paul Maddern was born in Bermuda of Irish and Cornish stock. After stints in Denver, San Francisco and London, he moved to Co. Down in 2000. He is currently completing a PhD at the Seamus Heaney Centre, Queen's University Belfast, which involves establishing a digital archive of public poetry readings. In 2006 he was awarded the James Kilfedder Bursary and was selected for Poetry Ireland's Introductions reading series. He is a winner of the Templar Poetry Pamphlet Prize 2009 and the resulting pamphlet, *Kelpdings*, is forthcoming.

Counterpoint

after Conor O'Callaghan

Place something on the windowsill
before we get to swallows in the evening sky,
something between you and the sovereignty of air:
week-old roses, silver-framed relations,
or an old milk jug, chipped Cornish ware.
You choose, but it should be noted
as you're opening the mail, look up,
and make a little from the fact it's framed
by more than fabric: hand-washed nets become
the history of lace as it pertains to family,
or in that vein, the fading luxuries of velvets.
And as the swallows flit, of course like memories,
here you'll neatly segue to your close,
recall old dialogues, spot the stranger passing.

Bodysurf

for Erin

To understand everything about the swell—
how on a given day the seventh in the cycle
provides the greatest chance to ride to shore
if caught where the rip collides with the surge,
where the wave pries a mouth wide
and prepares to heave its travelled miles—
to understand the moment of submission,
when to dive in and up the crest
in order to avoid a rabid tumble,
flung skyward out the other side
falling yards into the trough and humbled—
to understand that we're aligned
to leave behind horizons to the climbing wall,
hunched and turned three quarters,
believing that the travelling momentum
is such we'll be absorbed and pulled along,
so someone watching oceans from a towel
might raise herself a little on one elbow
and to her partner whisper, *Dolphins.*

The Beachcomber's Report

The best place to hear the ocean in a shell
is at a plain wooden desk in a bare room,
your eyes closed, knowing that if open
they would overlook the sound
you're trying to remember.

If you're on a beach checking driftwood
for texture, density and weight, stop.
Take the pieces to the fireside and just before burning
smell them, then rub your index finger along the grain.
that's when you will value their assets best.

When you pick up an imperfect green glass
lobsterpot float, carry it to a distant beach
where such things do not exist and drop it
implausibly beyond the high-tide mark
for locals to puzzle over.

Barbie heads, Ken torsos, Cabbage Patch fingers
are best buried in identikit suburban yards,
forgotten, save for a vague feeling
a writer might one day dig a bed for roses
and imagine non-existent children.

Should you retrieve the message from the bottle,
hide the note in a library frequented by academics,
within a dry encyclopaedia—
Biographie Générale. 35-36, Mer-Mur?
Check from time to time if it has disappeared.

Collect frayed orange nylon rope
and pay someone who knits the going rate
for a sackcloth-and-ashes jumper;
ideal for sitting in that bare room
listening for the ocean in a shell.

And when all of this has been accomplished
burn the desk, scatter the driftwood cinders,
throw all floats and doll parts back to the sea,
unravel the jumper, and travel to Bermuda
primed to search for Prospero's Book.

Retreat

I've built us a house from hand-cut limestone
and stacked the blocks without mortar.
Accrued weight is the only chance they'll get.

Our floorboards are of rare untreated cedar,
pegged and laid over bleached coral sand.
I'll leave you to ponder the benefits of staining.

I've forgone electricity, opting to hoard
two hundred boxes of slow-burning candles, ten to a box.
Wood for the oven is drying out against the beach wall.

The oven is functional, the cooler exotically stocked.
In the dining room is a painted table with only two chairs.
Follow the logic: there's one queen-size in the one bedroom.

And propriety needs me to report there's no glass
in the window frames: what you thought
you saw through so clearly was, is, air. Say 'Ah....'

I'll bring my wardrobe, if you care to dress for dinner,
but there are no mirrors anywhere, of any kind,
no reflective surfaces of any sort. Like this, I will be fine.

I've had the roof lime-washed to the point
where rainwater is sufficiently filtered
to provide the softest supply for bubble baths.

That lofty ambition complete, I've tried out some names:
Cove Edge, Beachcomber's Hut, Blue Horizons.
But at this time of life, and given our circumstance,

let's live with the sign on the gate: KEEP OUT! *Renaissance.*

On Being Told by an Irishman
that I Overuse 'Oleander'

If I agree, will you then permit me the use of avocado, mango,
    palmetto, Sargasso, wahoo,
pompano, lagoon, pedalo, lilo, longtail, mangrove, grotto, coral,
    and cahow (the word we
gave the only indigenous creature to be found on our small
    island), bougainvillea, poinciana,
pawpaw, cassava, casuarina, barracuda, bermudiana, (a tiny wild
    iris that is almost an
adjective), frangipani, amaryllis, kiskadee, cereus, but most of all
    cedar? Can I keep cedar?
Because we have a strain of cedar that like the cahow is
    indigenous to our island and to
which we have given our island's name. And this cedar, the most
    fragrant of cedars, deep
grained, producing oils, is in danger. It was once the bronzed
    bones of whalers and dinghies,
and prize-seeking sloops that outstripped what the world had to
    offer. And while it played its
part in the fabric of flogging posts, gibbets, stocks, stakes and
    pyres, when the blight of '46
destroyed almost all the trees, our island mourned. We still
    mourn and preserve what
remains. Today, for example, it is a sin to burn cedar as firewood.
    Instead we admire its
antique nature, found in the ceiling-beams and box-pews of St.
    Peters (the oldest Anglican
church in the Western Hemisphere), in ceremonial chairs and
    boardroom tables, the banisters
of grand staircases, dressers, sideboards, linen chests, captains'
    chests, window- picture- and
bed-frames and a few surviving household items: fruit bowls,

      butter-paddles, drinking cups,
lace bobbins, even knitting needles, crotchet hooks and
      toothpicks. Can I keep cedar? You
see:

        wise men are surplus

        we've allspice, oleander

        our cribs are cedar.

But if I agree, perhaps you'll reimburse us by giving up words
      that are losing their appeal:
linnet, blackbird, whin, swan, salmon, waterfall, lough, ashling,
      angelus, cottage, bog, spade,
hunger, potato, wheaten, farl, fiddle, father, mother, tongue,
      holy, relic, saint, shroud, shawl,
cairn, tower, united, North, South, border, colony, and while I'm
      about it can I thank you for
your Troubles?

NYARADZO MASUNDA

 Nyaradzo Masunda was born in Gutu district of Zimbabwe in 1972, the youngest of three children. Her father was a school teacher turned politician. Her mother was also a school teacher who gave up her job to join her husband after he was politically banned from teaching. Her father died when she was five months old. She was brought up by her mother who herself aspired to be a writer. Nyaradzo went on to study accountancy. However she kept her love for poetry close at heart. Nyaradzo came to Ireland to join her husband Lovemore Katsamudanga a Civil Engineer working in Cork. She has two children, Rutendo, eight, and Tino, five, both boys.

Walk My Walk

Before you walk my walk
Take my boots
Do you feel the tightness?
Do you feel the stones piercing through?
Do you feel the thorns?
This is the walk I walk

Before you talk my talk
Take my stage
Do you feel the nerves?
Do you feel their anticipation?
Do you feel my stammer?
This is the talk I talk

Before you sing my song
Take my heart

Do you feel my pain?
Do you feel my passion?
Do you feel my anger?
This is the song I sing

Before you cry my cry
Take my plight
Do you feel my desperation?
Do you feel my sorrow?
Do you feel my loss?
This is the cry I cry.

Land of Four Emotions

It's green and wet not for long
It's brown and grey not for long
It's cold and frosted not for long
It's dusty and windy not for long
It's a land of four emotions

I have treaded on her with bare feet
I have treaded on her with boots on
I have treaded on her in stilettos
I have also driven on
Roads rocky and dusty tarmac

I have slept on a reed-mat
I have slept under the stars
I have slept in three or four stars
No wonder that I am a wreck of emotions
Crying, laughing sometimes, but not for long

JENNIFER MATTHEWS

 Jennifer Matthews was born in Columbia, Missouri (USA) in 1976. After studying for the MA in Creative Writing at the University of Northumbria she moved to Cork, Ireland in 2003 and continues to live there now. Aside from book reviews for *Southword Journal*, she also writes poetry and has been published in *Mslexia, Revival* and *Poetry Salzburg*. Additionally, she recently read her work at the New Writers Showcase in the Heaventree Poetry Festival in Coventry, UK.

Panda

My girlfriends are surrounded by silks
and I am outside,
looking in on this library of femininity:
rolls of ruby and cherry blossoms,
cool sapphire dragon pools,
jade envy forests—
manuals to be chosen from
just beyond the stall of heady spices,
in the Duyun covered market.

I shuffle softly to hide my girth
behind a butcher block table
while the seamstress giggles,
fingertips to lips,
at the numbers that measure
my friends' willowy western lengths.
Their souvenirs: handmade Chi Paus—
dresses with slender, eastern cuts
which, while worn, will lend an instant
image of exoticness.

My souvenir: fear
of the tape wide
round my hips, my thighs,
my belly—
marking the size of
a true 'panda',
Chinese slang for 'westerner', or
the name of an animal
which is black-eyed, weary,
fumbling,
unnapproached,
unnapproaching.

Rootless

retelling Persephone

The poppy's lips promised escape,
a birth in reverse.
Its roots curled like beckoning fingers.

I plucked it, shaking
the clinging dirt from the roots
and the ground ripped open for me.

Through the gash a dark man came
and I dove into his river
to my marriage bed.

Neglect wintered the world behind me,
above me. My twin-mother's grief
took every living thing hostage.

Under world, I sucked pulpy seeds,
nails hooked in the rind of my husband's fruit,
juice seeping in sordid rivers down my chin.

Witnesses would return
to advise her-
this was no kidnapping.

CLARE McDONNELL

Clare McDonnell was born in London in 1937, of an Irish father and an English mother. As a child she was evacuated to relations in counties Kilkenny and Carlow during the Second World War, and spent every holiday of her life thereafter in her beloved Ireland. Clare came to live here permanently in 1971, when she married an Irishman, and has been in Co. Donegal since 1978. She is a widow with two grown up daughters. Her poetry has been published in many journals and anthologies, including *The Kent and Sussex Poetry Folio, Poetry Ireland Review, The SHOp, Leitir* and *The Cork Examiner*. Clare is a founder member of the *Errigal Writers*, and obtained an M.A. from Lancaster University, through the Poet's House, Falcarragh, Co. Donegal. Her first collection of poetry, *Feeling for Infinity*, was published by Summer Palace Press in 2006.

A Betting Man

I should have known
when he told me the story
of the kittens, and laughed.
His father was a betting man too.

He ruined his mare for a bet.
Something about a cart
loaded to the hilt with corn
and the steepest hill in the area.

Whether the bet was won
by his mare or his neighbour's,

I don't know.
But about the kittens—

I should have known
when he found it so amusing,
that bet on the kittens,
kittens in a bucket of water.

Breakfast with Salvador Dali

I could see right through him
as he arrived on a row of bicycles.
He wanted something to eat.

He helped me cook pancake
watches, and tossed them
all over the kitchen.

They drooped over
the backs of chairs,
over branches of trees

and dead fish, they slithered
off the edge of the table.
He shaped butter and bread

into buttocks and breasts,
with legs in strange places.
He ordered an egg on a

dish, without a dish,
and when I gave it to him
he hung it from the ceiling

on a rope. He looked
at the pancake watches
and said it was time to go.

But part of him didn't want to go,
so he left that part behind,
propped on a forked stick,

balanced over a shiny slice of water,
suspended like a hammock
from wall to invisible wall.

Drop

My boat
is motionless on
a looking-glass lake. A
drop of water, suspended from
the edge of the oar, holds a miniature
sun at its heart, an upside-down world where
time has stopped. Stopped: for as long as the
stillness between two beats of a moth's wing,
the silence between two notes of a thrush's
song. For as long, in the scale of things,
as we have inhabited this drop
of water, suspended from the
edge of the cosmos.

IRMA MENTO

 Irma Mento was born in 1998 (writing poetry instead of listening to a lecturer) but Pilar Alderete, who writes as Irma Mento, was born in 1975 in Valladolid, Spain. She works and lives in Galway "by choice and good luck". She lived in Ireland before, in 1996-7, moving to Canada from 1999-2003. She has also lived in Brazil and loves travelling, writing and talking to people in many languages. She is completely delighted that you are actually reading this. *¡Buen provecho!*

Honey

Jurek likes honey but not as a vocative
and I had learnt bad habits
I have deprived many words of their meanings,
chewed them up like gum
until they were tasteless.
These words, that once spat, stay stuck in our soles

stuck in our souls;
words we acquired or stole,
antiseptic.

Spanish Linguistic Variation

Variation 1

I am blending, borrowing words
from Medellín

from León
from Tescoco
from New York.

I'm mixing accents, intonations.
I'm blending, borrowing words,
fixed expressions, or not so

I'm paying an interest on them.

This is my rate:
Only when I speak to myself, I use my mother tongue.

Variation 2

My friend from Buenos Aires wants my Spanish.
I imitate la Habana. With no success.
I was never able to speak like in Malabo.
I'm seaweed in English waters.
I'm grafted. Spanish soil is elsewhere.
And how do you want me to teach you my Spanish?

If that language exists anywhere, it's inside of me.
Scuba-dive.
My Spanish borrows what is left
to say:

When I want to make a difference
I use the gypsy beat.
I think southern to myself.
The language you want me to teach you
I only use when I think aloud alone.

SUSAN MILLAR DuMARS

 Susan Millar DuMars was born in Philadelphia in 1966. Her mother is from Belfast, her father from Pennsylvania. She has lived in Galway, Ireland since 1998. Her poetry and fiction have been published in Ireland, Britain, the US and continental Europe. Her first poetry collection, *Big Pink Umbrella*, was published by Salmon Poetry in 2008. A second, *Dreams for Breakfast*, will appear in 2010. One of her poems will be featured in the Munster Literature Centre's *Best of Irish Poetry, 2010*. Her fiction was showcased in *American Girls* (Lapwing Press, 2007). She has been the recipient of an Irish Arts Council Bursary. A dedicated creative writing teacher, her essay "What's the Point?" featured in Salmon's 2009 *Poetry: Reading It, Writing It, Publishing It*. Together with her husband Kevin Higgins she has organised the Over the Edge readings series in Galway since 2003.

Part of Me

…is here amidst the glasses
and shiny hardback covers, part of me toys
with my fork and orders the watercress soup,
smiles
into the blue evening, white sails caterpillared across the Marina.
Part of me blinks at the TV actor,
the singer-songwriter, the Nobel Laureate.
Every conversation is a Gerber daisy,
opening to the sun.
Here in my lace shawl,
legs swinging
beneath the heavy tablecloth;
the child allowed at the grownups' table.

Part of me is here by the grace of God
and good people, friends in common,
amidst the thick perfume
of coffee and cleverness.
Success is a white
stranger on the stairs
who might, or might not,
be beckoning.

Part of me is still
at home in silence,
thin smoke drifting
from an extinguished candle.
My toes curled in damp socks,
the bed a tattered raft.
Part of me makes instant anything,
envies the microwave bulb
its definite glare,
wonders if I'm still emitting
any rays at all.
Mutes the phone
so when it doesn't ring
it is only part of my plan.
Part of me
talks to myself
about waiting for buses
that never come;
avoids sitting
in your empty chair.

And wherever you are,
how ever many people
slurp your words, and
pat your back;

how ever many hulking cars
line the curb, waiting to take you
anywhere you want to go…
part of me is always
climbing in beside you.

And part of me is always
somewhere else.

Daughter

> *There is no more sombre enemy of good art*
> *than the pram in the hall.*—*Cyril Connolly*

You are such a quiet child,
muddy, soft,
still part animal;
kneeling in the back yard
wielding a plastic spade,
chewing your bottom lip.
Un-earthing worms.
Stripes of dirt under your nails.
Your head just a little
too big for your body.
Your jacket Christmas red.

Letters make words, lines, music—
you.
I close the book.
You are unmade.
The chance we couldn't take.

The plastic spade vanishes.
The child who would only wail
if I tried to work on a poem.
The hole in the back yard fills.
Your muddy tracks on the kitchen floor peel away.

I'm not sure I'm big enough
to hold the words and you—
you would suffer
for my smallness.

Your red jacket fades into cold cloud.
The fragrance of your hair becomes
the scent of promised rain.
The worms burrow, undisturbed.

Going At It

Saturday's trinity:
clothesline, lawnmower, sink.
A new ache in my back.
Mr. H. blows me a kiss.
I feel it land; flutter
like a moth against my neck.

Our neighbour's mouth is stuck
in permanent "O".
"Mrs. H! Did you see them?
Three o'clock this morning!
Young couple on the green,
going at it!"

She happened to look
out her bedroom window.
Her face is flushed, her hands fisted.
"The wretch's arms thrown open
like Jesus on the cross.
Shameless!
I should've phoned the Guards."

I bite my lip, remember
our first summer;
the night I lifted my dress
in Father Burke Park.
The scrabbly grass, his sudden
cool flesh. Who watched, I wonder,
from which dark window...
how long ago?

How long have I been this housewife
who hangs laundry as it grows dark?
And when was the last time I asked Mr. H.
to take a walk in the park?

JUDITH MOK

Judith Mok was born in Holland in 1963 and now lives in Dublin. She has published three books of poetry and two novels in Dutch and one novel and a short story in English. She has written numerous articles for RTÉ, *The Sunday Independent* and *The Irish Times*. Her career as a classical singer has taken her around the world.

Amsterdam

How do you remember a city
When yours is the flight of a bird?
In a white span of wings
You drew lines in the frozen light
Describing somebody's dream
Without noticing

While the houses stood empty and over-lit
Along the grim winter mirror called *gracht*
You flew your fading shadow—
Maybe catching the only ray of sunshine—
Over the bridges and into somebody's dream
Again: without noticing

They had names for you
Ground from a harsh alphabet
The bread was plentiful-
But the heart in the giving hands
Was cold and needed to be fed—just like you—
Fed with a dream that went unnoticed
While you flew out to sea

And you tasted the cracked salt
On your beak again
And you let your sharp eye
Cleave the waves
In search of a silverfish.

Make or Break

They are standing in a Dublin vegetable shop;
Castanea Dentata, chestnuts said she,
Fauchon, remembering Paris, *Marrons Glaces:*
The faded butterfly wings of the wrapping paper
The box, half-open, like a promising, sweet smile
Her fingers reaching out for what her tongue would like: love.

We Irish, said he, play Conkers.

Stains

The gods of Babel went quiet
When I knelt down and begged for a translation.
So sure was I that every stain on your mouth
Meant a word with some significance;
These stains were letters written in deep crimson
Emphasized by a bright bloodied background,
An uneven lipped alphabet that was displayed
For my desire to decipher and read:
This is it, this is what I mean——you mean
That I came to believe in the truth of those stains
And forgot to turn back towards the light
Where my poems lay waiting for you

PANCHALI MUKHERJI

Panchali Mukherji was born in Calcutta, India. She was educated in New Delhi and the USA, and has obtained two Master's degrees, in Literature and Communications. At university she was elected president of the Creative Writing Society and organized literary workshops and other events for students. She has worked in advertising and as a qualitative research consultant, specializing in the analysis of consumer psychology. Her work has exposed her to diverse geographical and psychological landscapes and has also entailed extensive travel across India and other countries. She has an interest in communication arts, stimulated by early exposure to cinema, dance and other art forms in India. She has studied film making, and is engaged in developing scripts and ideas for documentaries. Panchali now resides in Dublin and is writing her first collection of poetry, as well as a book of poems for children.

The Passage of Time in a Teashop

Another smoky afternoon
With darkened eyes in corner rooms
Predictably, you and I
Scented Darjeeling
Slightly chipped china cups
The fog of talk
Complacent breasts
Rise and fall
In brittle laughs
And at your shoulder greybeard strikes
Anew a flaming match
And on the wall a poster flaps.

And every table owes a bill
And every chair has had its day
These lanterns cast a half life glow
Now the ching of brass ringed tills
Fill coffers with their fleeting vows

And you ask me how I pass my time,
Your coral rings astrological—
These lanterns swing like
Pendulums,
I say
And with their implacable sway
They push my days into
The night.

And now you look the other way.

Odysseus Today

The scan reveals so little
the bones of a lifetime
laid out
for unreliable examination
senses dulled
deliberately
the glass now empty and sticky
the eyes half open
memories float by
suffusing this evening
with a veracity of sorts
even in their blatant
imaginings

so you had a design
it was meant
not to be
a plan to leave before
you arrived, a convincing
exit
a red stick figure always running

but then you entered
this labyrinth
this profusion of late jasmine
this balmy night of eternal summer

clouds float yellow against the black moon

and you are slowly becalmed
losing your pre-determined way

stay, whisper the trees
stay.

MARY MULLEN

Mary Mullen's great-grandparents (Ryan, Day, Maher, Massey, McNamara) left Ireland at the time of the Great Famine. Her parents, Marge and Frank Mullen, left Chicago after World War II and availed of land offered to veterans 'out west' under the Homestead Act. They chose a piece of land in Soldotna, 150 miles south of Anchorage, Alaska, where Mary, the youngest of four children, was born in 1952. She moved to Ballinderreen, Co. Galway in 1996, where she still lives with her daughter, Lily. She has been published in literary journals and newspapers on both sides of the Atlantic. She has finished a poetry manuscript, is writing a memoir, and teaches a memoir class. Most days she wonders if the circle of life will bring her and Lily back to Alaska, "a place so startling she can't shake it loose".

Atlas

Unlike some of your friends
who were born with Down syndrome,
you had no bowels to be stitched,
no heart needing repair, no intestinal blockages.
You were my lucky Lily
but then icicles dripped in the spring thaw.

First, tiny tear ducts syringed.
Second, a grommet inserted in minuscule ear.
Third, tear ducts syringed, again.
Forth, tonsils and adenoids removed.
Fifth, another grommet for each faintly finer ear.

Five times they stuck in the cannula,
dressed you in a tiny gown with teddies.
Five times I sang to you while the anaesthetist
put mask over heart-shaped lips.
Five times you went limp,
disappeared behind sterile doors.

Five times I shuffled down the hall
tried to read, write. Stand. Sit.
Questioned my faith then prayed.
Minutes gonged. Thirty-five, forty-two
"She's not quite awake."
Forty six, forty seven, forty eight.

Then you gave a groggy smile.
I stroked your baby body,
cooed at my broken bird.
A nurse stood by you while I ran
down three flights of stairs,
inserted eight warm coins into filthy phone
told my mother in Alaska
"Lily's fine, just fine, fine."
Me too, I lied.

I wanted the icicle to stop dripping
so we could shut the hospital door
make friends with people who were not doctors
find someone who could hold up half the sky,
just once.

Your Cells Ache

When you are uprooted your cells ache
for the familiarity of frost on your beard,
desert sand in your ears, the hack of a machete
on breadfruit, or the rattle of your neighbour's truck
signifying work well done. Uprooted, you miss
the gush of the creek over pee yellow snow
and the steady positioning of stars
that have taught you everything you know.

Your cells ache for the heat of the arm
that reaches to pick up the baby,
or the knock on the hut from an old man
who made you dandelion tea.
Your cells search for that familiar face
who knows that people with your surname
read the mountains before they fish
for marlin or slap dirty clothes on rocks.

You were unearthed by fancy, seduced
by prospect. Hammered by persecution.
Or, perhaps you just knew too much.
You are constantly affronted by music
unknown to your womb, hounded by puffy white bread,
puzzled by unnecessary *u*'s stuck between an *o* and a consonant,
bothered by people who chat about the weather
while you long for words thicker than *'Tis a lovely day'*.

Now your cells desperately dig
but there is no loam in the west,
only whitethorn sculpted eastward
that cling to a slippery moonscape.

You realise this homelessness will kill you
the way the jolt of a shovel on a raspberry runner
kills the shoot but not the main plant.
In the face of immeasurable daily pain
you call the wind to gust you towards
the red raspberries, the hats on a hook;
earth you in the homeland garden, sow you
close to the forget-me-nots who did remember.

PETE MULLINEAUX

 Pete Mullineaux (b.1951) grew up in Bristol, UK, where, when he was 13, his poem 'Harvest Festival' was chosen for Macmillan's anthology, *Poetry & Song* and recorded on vinyl by Harrap. In the late 70s he joined London punk-rock band The Resisters, before going solo as singer-songwriter/poet, Pete Zero, playing gigs from Trafalgar Square to Glastonbury, alongside such luminaries as The Pogues. He won the City of London poetry/song contest, appeared in Apples & Snake's anthology, *Raw & Biting Cabaret Poetry*, (Pluto Press, 1984) and along the way received a first class honours in Drama from Middlesex University. In 1991 he moved with his Irish partner and daughter to Galway, where he works in drama, creative writing and development education. A number of plays have been produced for stage and RTÉ radio and for several years he has hosted the Cúirt International Festival of Literature Poetry Slam. In 2005 Belfast's Lapwing Press published a chapbook, *Zen Traffic Lights*, and finally in 2008 Salmon Poetry released his first full-length collection, *A Father's Day*.

Wasting Away

We hope that some things cannot be erased,
(the Buddhist sees each sorry soul return)
though most of it will have to go to waste.

Hooked on progress, forever making haste
we gobble up, incinerate and burn;
believing some things cannot be erased.

And from fearing we may become debased,
we cultivate improvement; seek to learn:
though most of it will have to go to waste.

But whether we're the chaser or the chased,
much like a coin, depending on the turn—
hoping that some things cannot be erased

we look back at those footprints barely paced;
ley lines of meaning wistfully discern...
though most of it will have to go to waste.

Thinking then of this life as but a taste
of things to come; beyond current concern:
accepting we *will* one day be erased—
we hope (and pray) that some things never go to waste.

Playing Boats
for Cassie

Running for the river
she barely breaks her stride
to pluck a yellow dandelion;
while I take time to choose
a broad, tapering leaf—
not too green.

And here we come!
her in front, approaching the first fall.
Down...under; then up she bobs—
snags on a rock
while I career on into calmer waters.

But then she's wriggling, and free!
Rotating, gathering momentum
until we're finally neck and neck—
father and daughter, sailing up the Nile, the Amazon.

A whirlpool—
now I'm in difficulties
taking in water, while she shoots clear.
We watch, cheek to cheek
until her yellow head disappears
beneath overhanging trees...

Am I sad my boat sank? She asks.

The rules are simple: if both get stuck
we throw stones to dislodge ourselves
or run ahead, removing obstacles.
But what if one fails to make the start:
will our game not then be over?

Come on, she coaxes, chiding
my dark cloud, swiping another flower
holding it under my chin.

This time I seek a fresher,
more robust leaf.
Best of three, I say—
let's see that dandelion spin!

TOM MYP

Tom Myp was born on December 6, 1943, during the darkest years of what the Russians term The Great Patriotic War, on the Pacific island of Svyataya Yekaterina. His father, a construction engineer, was one of the first to work the goldfields of southern Ethiopia, where he was at one point joined by his family, and they and he later spent many years in the Middle East, where he attended an English-language school in Beirut. A host of experiences followed this formative period, including travel to and in the US and different countries in Asia and Europe, culminating in his move for good from Russia to Ireland in 1995 with his wife and stepson. All three are Irish citizens, and Myp feels particularly close to County Sligo and its music and environs.

The Universal Difference

In the universe of answers to
the universe of questions,
just the one recurs: "No,
no: you can't go home."

So choose it carefully as you can:
the universe your son will shrug away,
the universe your daughter flees.

Two Words on the Subject of Autumn in Russia

Pitch all your autumnal,
evening tones together:
cello-like, long hooting drones
absent anything but remorse to
lever your thoughts inexorably
'round to blind snow,

interminable.

Grew stupid in exile, you did; now you
roost like some bedraggled bird
undone by its own instinct,
strayed from the migratory
template, and wonder how you've come
'round to this grief, this melancholy.

CHRIS NIKKEL

 Chris Nikkel was born in Canada, in 1977. He grew up in the province of Manitoba, in the prairies, where he studied at the University of Winnipeg before going on to pursue a Masters of Fine Arts in Creative Writing from the University of British Columbia, in Vancouver. He first came to Ireland in 2003 to be with his partner in Galway, and then moved with her to Belfast in 2006. His poetry has appeared in journals and magazines in both Ireland and Canada. In 2005 he was awarded first prize in the "Great Canadian Love Poem" competition. In addition to poetry, he writes narrative non-fiction and works as a documentary screenwriter for Five Door Films. He was born of Mennonite heritage, a tight-knit cultural group known for its communal lifestyle and pacifist beliefs. There are Mennonite communities all over the world, but they traditionally claim no homeland.

Dandelion Wine

Grandma shaved kindling for fires as a child
peels skin off buttered stalks of dandelion.

And while the Russian kids learned of vodka
and class and the swindling habits

of Mennonites, she ladled cabbage borscht,
baked bread for her brothers and boiled

plums picked from their many fruit trees
sprawling too close to the village. *Careful*

next to the flame, you'll burn the crust,
her mother nagged, shoving another pan beside

the coals. Stalin had by then sent for his trains.
I have a photo: grandma balanced on the fender

of the only car in the district. Her skirt's
neatly hemmed, shoes gleaming as they dangle.

She never talked about the wealth.
Spoke only of pickling spice

and the wine she'd made from rotten fruit
and wilting heads of dandelion.

For Those That Stay

Not much left of the Crimean homestead.
A few scattered roof-tiles. The odd red

brick from the old barn, disappearing
in the dirt. And the German round-well

open-mouthed and hazardous in a corn field,
bones of fallen goats and the town rubbish

dumped down its water-hole. Spun in brittle
blocks quarried a mile up the road, it waits,

stone lip grown over with age. Grandma
grew up hearing the whine of the saws

shaving stone to square. No birdsong,
no music pierced the kitchen window

as she pickled overripe pears. Then saws
switched to gunshot, jars rattling the shelves.

Her father walked calmly from the field,
wiped his hands in a hanky. Then

the car sputtered outside the door.
She took the last train to the Black Sea,

boarded ship to Montreal, another
train to the hinterlands: Manitoba,

Siberia—an exile for some,
home for those that stayed.

You Said

Yesterday we drove up the coast. Head in map,
I charted our way, kept a vigil for risk.

You muscled around corners as mountains
seemed to elbow out to sea. Is this love?

How cliffs carved from water still connect
to the depths? And us caught between,

pinned to death to keep us from peril.
You said, braking: *isn't it strange, we are*

all of us nomads, tracing back. I'm Irish—
everyone's Irish all over the world.

And though my roaming was as homeless,
and yours from homesick, we both found

the corners of this earth, pace the edge of the same
tilled field. Now we wring dirt with our fingers,

extending aging hands to new potatoes
as to a drowning man gulping saltwater in the surf.

So, maybe the heart's not the only organ keeping us
alive. Perhaps it's our feet that flutter when they need,

sidestepping danger to carry us through
until we're carried away a last time.

DANIEL O'DONOGHUE

Daniel O'Donoghue was born on the Rosslare-Fishguard ferry on October the twenty fifth 1953. He has never been clear about which direction the boat was travelling in, but applying the old three-mile limit he has about an 89% chance of having been born in international waters. In 2006 he was asked to translate some of Salome de Luria's poems into Spanish, and enjoyed the task so much that the momentum caused him to write a few of his own. The vein was soon exhausted however, and he no longer writes anything other than quite frankly scabrous memoirs. He has spent most of his life trying to learn music and languages, with varying degrees of success. In 2007 he arranged the Grammy nominated CD *Ka Hikina o ka Hau* for Dancing Cat records. In 2008 he published extracts translated from the infamous racist Arthur Gobineau's *Trois ans en Asie* and *Religions et Philosophies dans l'Asie Centrale* with Routledge.

Cycle

Eiffel tower view
Accordion plays musette
We know where we are

Horseflies, mosquitoes,
the shortest night of the year
Why did we come here?

Leaves fall silently
Great tree veins the harvest moon
Who will say goodbye?

Frozen lake beckons
with clear path to journey's end,
but stay where you are

O Tera 2 (the temple)

My foot stops short of total destruction
The world's smallest frog doesn't know what she's missed
nor that somewhere
in a land she has never heard of
she is a symbol of something called "fertility"
Away she hops
I miss her
It was long ago
and far from the fertile valley of the Nile.

Mariposa

> *(to nobody in particular, except perhaps Leopardi*
> *and Gonzalo's metronome)*

My grandmother used to tell me
the ticking of the clock kept her company
in bed.

tick tock

I found it very sad
I don't have a clock but
many are the times and more

tick tock

tick tock

my only reason
for being alive
is to keep the fire going
that keeps me warm
and the butterfly that hibernates
on the ceiling of the bedroom
where I never sleep

tick tock
tick tock

tick tock

ab initio
ad infinitum

KINGA OLSZEWSKA

 Kinga Olszewska was born in Poland, in 1975 in the beautiful medieval city Toru. She is, in the words of the Polish poet Stanisław Barańczak, "a Pole living abroad". She came to live in Ireland almost ten years ago to pursue a PhD in Arts and has been at home in Galway since. She has travelled widely and speaks a few languages but writes in only one—English. For a number of years she was involved in interpreting for Galway Community Services which made her aware of the difficulties and prejudices faced by immigrants. Some of her poems have been inspired by her work as an interpreter.

Site for Sale

'Site for sale to locals in the area'
I go in to inquire.
Are you local? the man behind the desk asks disbelievingly.
I have been local for the last ten years.
But you are not really Irish?
So I recite: Irish passport, Revenue, Hibernian, Bank of Ireland,
Áine and Saoirse, holiday house in Wicklow,
I start quoting national heroes
When the man interrupts
In fairness, I don't think it's a site for you.

Despite economic downturn,
In Ireland, business as usual.

A Sort of Homecoming

I'm back.
I shed my winter skin, my big boots, coat and woolly hat
Scarf defrosting my vocal cords so I can
Still hear the sound of my rustling tongue
I fold them carefully and lovingly and put them on the top shelf
Because I don't need them where I am now.
The first few days I read a lot
I think a lot
Evoke the images
         the sounds
            the shapes
That were once so inseparable from me.
I nervously pick up the phone
Hoping to hear a voice whispering
That the Atlantis I so recklessly renounced
Has not been drawn yet.

A Letter

Dear Félix and Giles,
When I read your famed piece, I immediately started making preparations:
Sold the house, said goodbye to family,
Closed bank accounts and got a good pair of shoes.
After all, exploring on horseback or by public transport is so *passé*.

I inhaled deeply and thought:
Hail eternal freedom!
Hail struggle against the system!
Death to rules, regimes and laws!
Viva the war machine!

I could just picture myself:
I am no citizen, my skin polychromatic.
I am multiplicity incarnated!
My power cannot be measured in Pascals.
I am pure *potentia*.

And then I saw them
Men, women and children wheeling their existence among sealed and cool interiors,
And poverty-proof minds,
Travellers moved like pawns on a republican chessboard.

I understood that *e pluribus unum* was the highest form of integration,
That prayers in your mother tongue triggered ethnic divides,
And that neutrality could also be a form of totalitarianism.

I saw that nomads and people of colour
Did not construct their war machines, as you predicted,

For their neighbours and airport officers kept a close watch.

And, to be quite honest,
I did think of a different planet
Where we could all finish building our Urgemeinschaft.

But, really, Félix and Giles,
Is this incessant movement absolutely necessary?
Can we just not rest?

JULIA PIERA

Julia Piera was born in Madrid in 1970. She studied Economics and Art in Madrid, Bolonia and Brighton, and holds a Masters in Romance Languages and Literatures from Harvard University. In addition to her work for *El viajero* of *El País,* she has published the poetry collections *Al vértice de la arena* (Biblioteca Nueva, 2003), *Conversaciones con Mary Shelley* (Icaria, 2006) and *Puerto Rico Digital* (Bartleby, 2009). She lives in Dublin where she is currently the director of Instituto Cervantes in Ireland.

Bamboo Time

> *to Nuria, in the hammam at Molenbeek, and to Farida*

We go into and out of the steam.

The steam drips,
covers vertical time.

To weigh less,
to talk less

to be slow
like our bodies,
to write the passage of the seasons
in oils of almond and sandalwood.

*

They laugh, the ladies of the baths. Strangers
to the city outside, to its solid rain,
they teach painted hands, naked languages,
tongues of the south, touches of moving balm
necks, arms, bellies,
the tingling of rose and pepper unguents

cinnamon between our fingers
steam above our lives

above our bodies, steam.

*

we go into and out of the steam

to be slow,
to talk less,
to weigh less,

to listen to the bamboo time
and to await the flowering
in both worlds
once,
every two hundred years.

Translated by David Butler.

Glass Serpent

I can absorb water
through my skin,
collect rain, accumulate dew.

I can see contours with my eyes
which simulate clouds
and look at myself in the mirage
of a well.

I can unfurl my body
into forming ample waves
with grains of sand.

But I will not fly,
nor can I emigrate,
nor will I find my grave in the sea
when the springs run dry
and the remains of ponds and lakes evaporate.

Self-Portrait of the Invisible Woman

In this land with no shadow
that any touch of sun
inflames with void
I do and undo spirals
as my only trade
and as my only fancy
I feel my body shrink
inch by inch,
proportionally,
to the rhythm of the sand's pulse.

*

The sand crunches.

My hands crack, dry,
they droop with the weight of time
and I give myself up to a thing
which concludes for me.

*

This is a portable land
made only of windows.

Without anniversary.

Translated by Andrea Bachner

HAJO QUADE

Hajo Quade was born in 1956 in Darmstadt, Germany. He studied social work in Freiburg in the Black Forest before moving to Ireland in 1989. He lives in Galway where he works as a translator. In 2008 he was runner-up in the Over The Edge New Writer of the Year competition.

For Kevin

I took the stone from my pocket
A brimming pitch black oval
With summer island memories
Silently sliding it onto the pillow
Beside your ashen head
Whishing it might keep you warm

Hoping you would dream the sea

Next time I saw you
The sick-house busy
I did not ask about your dream
I did not even ask about the pebble stone
Instead
You smiled at me
And both of us knew that it was time to go

I sometimes return
The Crane, on Sunday afternoon
Your laughter and your music
Ringing in my ears
Behind the counter

On the far side of the room

When Pat decides to play a tune of yours
Your smile starts weaving soon
Across the echo of his strings

Vibrating from the far side of your room

The Crow

Death came for a visit
This fine spring morning
Outside the window of my living-room

Swaying on a naked branch
In the bush with the blood red foliage
Turning over new leaves

He took time out
From working hard these days
On the body language of my friends
Soaking-up the sun
And defending his territory

I fed him breadcrumbs from my plate

Even death needs a breather

Time Warp

I would peel time back
Banish apples from the heavenly garden
Meddling with God
So I'd know
If peaches were just as tempting

I would peel time back
Bag butterflies, in Camus bog, with Beckett
Conceiving a chaos theorem in Connemara
So I'd know
The nature of my cold feet

I would peel time back
Have me a year of groundhog days
When it is spring, and I'm in your arms again
Even knowing, that,
When I'm slowly drowsing into the realm of darkness,
I hear Orpheus singing our swan song

And

I would peel time back

URSULA RANI SARMA

 Of Irish/Indian descent, Ursula Rani Sarma was born in Canada in 1978 and grew up in the West of Ireland. Ursula has written predominantly for the theatre since completing her BA at UCC in 1999. Her award-winning plays have been translated, performed and published extensively, both at home and abroad and include *Touched, Blue, Orpheus Road, When the War Came, The Spidermen, The Magic Tree* and *The Exchange*. These plays were commissioned by companies such as the National Theatre London, Paines Plough Theatre London, the Traverse Theatre Edinburgh, the Stephen Joseph Theatre Scarborough and The Abbey Theatre Dublin amongst others. Ursula co-founded Djinn Theatre Company in 1999 and has directed several productions as Artistic Director. She holds an MPhil from Trinity College Dublin and has been Writer in Residence for several companies including the Royal National Theatre London, Paines Plough Theatre Company London and The Eugene O'Neill Theatre Centre. Awards for her work include Irish and British Arts Council Awards, an Irish Times ESB Theatre Award and an Edinburgh Fringe Festival Award.

Love Song

Write me a bird
He said
I can't fly this poem and neither can you
And what then shall we both do
Only fumble with the walkers and lift our heels
Beyond the grey matter
That seems, in this city
To cover not just shoes and coats

But hearts and minds too
Thoughts
Sentiments
Encased and embalmed
In all that is dull and grey and unforgivable.

Write me a bird
Long and white
Graceful like the morning light
With wings big enough for two
For us my love
For me and you.

London's Burning

London's burning
You said
So I stretched my limbs and unfolded by bones and reached for the
heat of the flames
But there was nothing
No warmth to be found
Only dull embers doused in milk
And matches with no place to strike themselves
And brigades without a spark in sight.

The thought did occur then
That you and I
Were North and South
Sun and snow
Bitter and sweet.

Fire and no fire at all.

Lament

I will never be a dancer
This I have come to realise
The earth shall curve and flex itself
Against its many shelved edges
But my torso will remain exact.

My breath will never search onwards
Waiting for the lightness of touch that is
The wonder and weight of driftwood
The light of the turning sill.

Splinters for Children

I NOAH

If Noah was a colour
He would be a rainbow
Difficult to pin down to just the one hue
His eyes somewhere between the light before a glacial melt
And those wondrous night skies over Canada
That no one can pronounce.

II EMMET

Just in a beat
The quiet comes
Plucked from tears and feathers

Pyjamas and milk teeth
The dark things outside
Expand to fill the gaps
Created by the sound
Of a tired child
All at once
Asleep.

III RUAIRÍ

The morning you were born
The sun rose as it always did
There were slow terrestrial moves
Creaks
Like hips jointing forward
Continents waltzing
Amazing beasts in the wild
And you
Like a beacon
Warm and bright
All that is good
In the morning light.

MARK ROPER

 Mark Roper was born in Derbyshire in 1951, and brought up in North London. He went to a boarding school in Surrey, to university in Reading and Oxford, lived and worked in Sussex, Swansea and other parts of London. In 1980 he moved to County Kilkenny with his partner Jane. At first they shared a cottage with friends, then bought a cottage of their own in Tobernabrone, where they've lived happily ever since. His collections include *The Hen Ark* (Peterloo/Salmon 1990), which won the 1992 Aldeburgh Prize for best first collection; *Catching The Light* (Peterloo/Lagan 1997); a chapbook, *The Home Fire* (Abbey Press 1998) and *Whereabouts* (Peterloo/Abbey Press 2005). He was Editor of Poetry Ireland for 1999. *Even So: New & Selected Poems* was published by the Dedalus Press in Autumn 2008.

Fields

At dusk I'm drawn to the back lane
to watch the new foal. It floats and folds
around its mother, a giddiness, an armful
of feathers spilling out of itself.

On the hedgerows the white flowers
glow as darkness thickens.
Trees have settled to their long tasks.
Fresh leaves start to harden.

Almost past the edge of hearing, making
their claim on the lateness, children call.
A sound like the memory of a sound.
A dog barks. A car comes and goes.

On the hill lights begin to appear.
Swallows reel through the field.
Horse and foal have wandered away
and are lost in a gather of shadow.

The foal taking its first delicate steps.
Elsewhere my mother taking her last.

Silence

In your room
you sit with Silence.

Just a few small things
beside you.

She's asked you to clear
some space for her.

She doesn't leave now
when we come in.

When we talk
she tries to interrupt.

You keep looking
across at her.

We can almost
see her too.

We too begin to fall
under her spell.

When we leave
she fills the room.

You gaze at her.
Gaze and gaze.

Crossing

They are queuing up
to take on water,

skimming the surface
of a small pool

to sip at
their own image,

filling their small tanks.
Soon they'll leave.

I'll keep my eyes
peeled for their return.

April. I might be
on the phone perhaps

when the first one
makes its way past

the narrow window.
I might be sitting

where I used to sit
and talk to you.

I'll watch the swallow
wander by, looking for

where it will know
its crossing complete.

Public

After they had removed your body
and after Ann had tidied the house,
one room was full of metal and rubber,
all the scaffolding needed to keep you up,
the cushions, alarm, frames, wheelchair,
bath-lift, special bed, hoist.
Props waiting for another stage.

It had been such a show. So public.
And you were such a private soul.
You who hated the show of any feeling.
As soon as they began to treat you,
as soon as they touched, you withdrew.
You'd never have said, but it's there in the photos,
that set of mouth, that puzzle in your eyes.

You lost the will to live, like a bird
whose broken wing gets mended
but which won't even try to fly again.
Wildness damaged by handling.
All that weakness on show, as you grew
more and more helpless. Unbearable,
really, never to be on your own.

So you hid, in the only place you could:
inside yourself. You left your face behind,
crawled deeper and deeper in.
Unable to find a quiet corner to die,
you tried to die inside yourself.
It took you a long time to manage.
It couldn't have been easy.

Distance

Though you can see for miles
across the lake to the mountain,
and though you can imagine
all that lies beyond, ridge
after ridge and the rivers
joining to make their slow,
swollen progress to the sea;
though you think you can say
how far the sunlight travels
to wash the ears of ivy
and make the hawkweed blaze,
to warm the stone's cold shoulder
and warm the wary heart;
though you think as you swim
how you used to swim with her,
how you'd lie on your backs
and press your feet together
and race each other back to shore;
though you've reached, you think,
some idea of distances involved,
how things are so far apart

yet one and the same—
it will be, you will find,
as nothing to the distance
opened by the loon's cry
that first night; and, in the wake
of that cry, the silence.

JUDY RUSSELL

 Judy Russell was born in London in July 1944. Her parents, both medics, spent the war years in London, their two other children having gone to America as refugees. The family was reunited in 1946 and lived south of London in what was then countryside. In 1961 Judy came to Ireland to study at Trinity, followed by seven years working in Dublin theatre. Marriage and children led to a move into the hills to tend a smallholding, make cheese and yoghurt, grow vegetables, raise chickens and ducks. In later years she's had more time for writing, co-wrote (with Margaret Coen) *Alias Sprog* which won second place in the P.J. O'Connor RTÉ radio drama awards; a play *You and Whose Army?* which was put on by Red Rua Company; and an unpublished book. She joined the Shed Poets two years ago, who meet weekly to read and workshop work in progress.

Hunter Gatherers

Drawn to the living water
and such elemental forms
as rock and wrack
we dare only the threshold
of the enigmatic deep,

wade in shallow waves
scooping up sea lettuce,
and frightening hermit crabs
who tug their borrowed homes
deeper into the sand.

At the base of the cliff
we bundle driftwood,
pocket smoothed jewels—
rose quartz, amethyst and jasper,
load shell bowls and feathers

into a salvaged bucket.
Crags strident with gulls
sprout tasty samphire
high above the crinkled sea
where drifting clumps of nets,

trawler trash,
and plastic, drowning snares
and deadly debris
slop on the tainted tide.

Guilty Secret

You told me once
that you felt most alive in wartime
aboard a cargo ship with two spies,

running the gauntlet of torpedoes
in the North Atlantic
salt spray in your hair.

When peace returned
with motherhood and apple pie
your world contracted

to petty parish squabbles,
darning socks and endless ironing,
a book propped up to liberate your mind,

feed dreams of future years
when children would be reared.
Oh there's the danger

not under skies raining bombs
but in the quiet disappointment of the laundry room
folding ambition sides to middle.

Leaving

A chipped yellow crane
plunges its iron neck
to forage the harbour mud,
Diggosaurus disgorging
dripping mouthfuls
into a gaping barge.

Figures on the seawall
above the rip-rap
wait in the morning sun.
Such friends I leave
hunka relations
true riches of the heart.

From the top deck
I watch cars trickle
like termites into the gaping hold.

So many crossings I've made
between the country of my birth
and the land of my heart.

*

Beech trees knee deep in corn,
giant rolls of hay,
hours of fields and towns
scroll by the carriage window.

Across the heaving sea
the crane will be still now
as the evening ferry docks.

ECKHARDT SCHMIDT

 Eckhardt Schmidt, born near Hamburg, Germany, in 1953, lives in his cottage near Letterkenny, Co. Donegal since 1990. For two decades he worked in the printing trade, mostly with ink-stained hands, but when technology underwent rapid changes, software being used rather than lead and awl, he dropped out of the business and made his work in gardens his profession—where he could get his hands "dirty" again. Even so his love for the printed word stuck with him, and he is an avid reader of novels, poetry and "anything beautiful in both German and English".

Rowan-Berries

The rowan-berries are red now,
soon they will be eaten.
Sometimes a single seed happens
to spring to new life again,
having travelled inside a berry
through an entire bird.
Presumably we are within a bird
at present. Hopefully we have
been pleasant to his taste.

At Sea in Monaghan

Monaghan, the capital of rain;
Kerbs becoming quays
With no ship waiting for me;
Flotsam of it all
Down the drain.

JO SLADE

 Jo Slade was born in England in 1952. She is a poet and painter and lives and works in Limerick. She is the author of four collections of poetry: *In Fields I Hear Them Sing* (Salmon, 1989); *The Vigilant One* (Salmon, 1994), which was nominated for the Irish Times/Aer Lingus Literature Prize; *Certain Octobers* (Editions Eireanna, Quimper France, 1997), a dual language English/French edition, which received a publication bursary from the Centre du Livre, Paris France and *City of Bridges* (Salmonpoetry, 2005.) She was nominated in 2003 for the 'Prix Evelyn Encelot', Écriture Prize, Maison des Écrivains, Paris. Her poems have been translated into French, Spanish, Romanian and Russian and she has been published in journals and anthologies in Ireland and abroad. In 2003/2004 she was Poet in Residence for Limerick Co. Council and in 2007 she was Writer in Residence at the Centre Culturel Irlandais, Paris, France. She has exhibited her paintings in Ireland and France.

Leaving

Porthole to an ocean.
One child doesn't want to go
he's throwing up
has locked the cabin door
says he'll smash the glass.

She takes him on her lap
holds him.
The ship wrenches from the pier.
She's staring out.
Someone's waving.
"Look Mam the pier is moving."

She holds him tight.
They're disappearing.
Home's back there
it's where we're leaving.

Time-Piece

In the wardrobe of my belonging
is a bearskin coat.
I've never worn it.
I must remember to take it out
have it altered to fit—
take a walk with the bear on my back.

I'd like to find him inside it
my great grandfather.
The clock wound back
so I could see him as he was.
His nimble fingers placing the pins
his musical ear timing the cogs
his eye like a moon in the ocular.

I'd like to walk across Europe
to Feldberg & climb to the top.
Sit with him looking out
on a snowy vista.
We'd talk about time & the clocks
he made & why he left
the house by the lake.

Why he never went back.
Why his bearskin coat
hangs in my house—
ghost of truth
no one speaks about.
Is his the mark on my poet face
why I'm always a stranger
from another place?

Letters to an Immigrant Poet

for Magda

I

Take care your heart does not corrode
with the ire of the city.
I have been there with its countless tongues
and its relentless hunger.
Don't be swallowed into the belly
of its utter requirements.

II

Trust me nothing is true
not even kindness which you cherish.
The city is a vortex of voices that cannot be heard
above the noise of machinery and alarms.
Their nascent terror rises.

III

Poets are ridiculed as they cling
to the railings of meaning.
They cry out to the river and walls
as if these would absorb feeling.
But stone and water will not bear witness.

IV

You were born in a foreign city
this is your badge you cannot remove it.
For a second I saw you as a child
but your eyes filled with years.
Sorrow enters the streets.
It sleeps in a corner covered with clothes
the ones you discarded -
garments of promise that kept out the cold.

V

Even now you slip like a shadow
between language and meaning.
They're waiting
to siphon the music from you.
I want to appeal to your mouth in snow
before it fills with whiteness.
Before ice grips it and that fragile warmth
the colour of cherries goes.

TIZIANA SOVERINO

Tiziana Soverino was born on 28th March 1985 in Asti, Italy, the third daughter of Rosa Alfarano and Nicola Soverino. After spending her childhood and adolescence in Piedmont, Italy, she moved to Ireland in 2004. She received a BA degree in Celtic Studies from University College Dublin in 2007. From 2007, she has been working as a tutor in Celtic Civilisation in the same institution. She is currently completing an M. Litt in Irish Folklore on the Feast of Saint John in University College Dublin.

Fragments of Meaning

Fragments of meaning
Swim into the ocean of my mind,
Splinters of glass
Which sometimes glitter as wonderful snow in the winter sun,
And other times break
Every single chord of my being.

Mutable as the weather
In a mountain resort,
As the sea,
As the world,
My life
Runs too fast,
Or too slow.

Like a stone thrown into water generates circles
of different dimensions,

The world outside
And myself
Meet endlessly,
Hide, collide,
And run together.

Every now and then I feel
Like a child with a newly-received kite,
Who cannot get hold of the string for too long,
So that the kite disappears and gets lost
Into the sky, which is so big
It surprises and frightens.

But every time
I see something new in the world around me,
I am enchanted by something I had forgotten,
A bird's wing beat,
A flower grown in the middle of a city,
Or a smile
That warms my heart
And gives me hope again.

Thousands of reasons to open my eyes again
And see the world in all its wonder,
Finding the strength in every little whisper that
surrounds me.

RAPHAEL JOSEF STACHNISS

 Raphael Josef Stachniss was born in Trier, Germany in 1967. He worked as an investigative journalist, human rights' campaigner, he was founding chairman of a Multicultural Centre and an association working for unemployed citizens. His visual art has exhibited in Germany and Ireland. He lived in Italy for 8 years and currently lives in Dublin.

No time, no interest

the lad
in the local grocery store
seems to work
on a street
in nyc
where customers
never return
the girl
in the cafe
saw me a hundred times
and knows i take
a double espresso
and a glass of water
in ten years
thousands of doubles
and a lake full of water
later
i probably
know her name
and we might talk
about the weather

the mothers
in school
wear invisible
burkas
and say
hello
now that my son
is in 4th class.

the kids
have friends
for 2 hours
and a half
on saturday
and a sleepover once
a year

i loved
the snow this year
it made
the people
talk
about something
tyres
traction
traffic delays
and when
does it hopefully
end and

those icy conditions
finally change
for the better.

The red cow

going out
in the cold
the wind
and the rain
searching for truth
for something
new and unknown
feels like
driving through
the red cow roundabout
in dublin
ireland
the very
first time

LISA STEPPE

 Lisa Steppe was born a few months before the outbreak of the Second World War in Germany. The child spent the last three years of the war in the Alsace. The borderland region, having been annexed first by Prussia and again by Hitler Germany, has a strong presence in her poems. She studied Linguistics in Heidelberg and Munich Universities, taught for fifteen years in a secondary school and was active in the peace and anti-nuclear movement. In 1984 she left Germany and moved to Ireland. Lisa Steppe has won the Listowel Bryan McMahon Short Story Award and was on the shortlist for the Hennessy Literary Award, the Francis Mac Manus Award and the Fish Short Story Prize. Her poems were winners in the Edgeworthtown and Boyle Poetry Competitions and she was placed on the shortlist for the Strokestown International Poetry Award. Her first collection of poetry *When the Wheathorses Die* was published by Summer Palace Press. Her German books are *Die Kasematte* and *Island,* a travelogue about Iceland republished in July, 2009.

When You Go West

Take your remedial teacher with you, the one
With the carrot-coloured hair, the freckled
Voice that he may lift you across the threshold
Of otherness telling the locals you are a migratory
Bird and that the west shall not bog you down but do
What it does to stragglers from the Americas,
Fin and humpback whales which do not pass the test
Of comeliness either or tortoises coming
In on their backs and which are brought ashore with care.

When you go west
May there be an *Adamsbaum* in the sky,
A turning point, an opening, a door into a feathered
Room that is fifteen miles wide and its length
Unaccounted for and takes your breath away
And its western end is the wall of the sea.

When you go west
May nine mermaids smile you in, nine young
Men shy as larks accompany you to the haunts
Of lizards and wizards and whinchats shall be
There and wide-eyed seals and far out a school of dolphins
And shoals and shoals and shoals of fish.

But when you go west
Make sure you carry a cure
For the sharks, the sharks, the sharks.

Moments in Time

Listen to the first note a bird sings at dawn.
Respond with a ringing sound. Listen
To the tide at Streedagh Strand working stone.
Listen to the horse whipstitching sand, the rider's
Shrill *jubilate*. Listen to the land, parts
Of a shell midden falling into the sea
As we fall in love. As we fall in love.
Walk inland, listen to the autumn leaves
Settling on tarmac, the lanugo of wet grass.
Touch tree. That much for moment one.

Moment two. Listen to great-grandmother -
On your father's side, the German side—

Skating on Lake Wannsee. It is December 1899.
Listen to her skates inflaming ice. Listen
To the coupling of ice and steel. Listen
To cold fire. Listen to your great-grandmother's
Stallion sire your granny's mare Lilly—
Again the granny on your father's side, the German side.
Don't be silly and weep. I said, listen.

Moment three. Listen to your mother
When she talks to the speckled filly
Somewhere on a *ferme* in the Alsace.
Maman is French and nine. The early autumn
Blooms gossamer and is divine.

The last moment. Listen to *maman*
When they tar and feather her, the 'tart
Who fucked the enemy'. It is 1945.
Listen to the silence of her body
At the brink, her body cleaving
Water, sink. Listen.

Sister

Will you stay awake, watch
Over me when I nightly
Descend to the camp,
The cellar of bones

Assorting, labelling the lot?
My back hurts, it is so damp
Down here and I have
Done it for decades.

The eye that mostly frightens
Me is the one above the door
When the exit sign dims,
Blacks out and I am

In that shroud of darkness,
Of purity. Oh sister, stay
Awake as the silence
Down here is so loud.

I do my slim work of labelling
Skulls, thread them on baler
Twine hung between two
Metal hooks in the wall.

In the dark I sense the skulls'
Slow swaying like pegged washing
And yes, I always wash
Them before giving them back

Their names. Oh sister,
And now I'm getting on, I'm
Getting old and who will
Do the work in my stead?

Across the Ruins in Bright Shoes

Remember when we ran into the evening
Shift, that gang of weirdos down at the river,
Human conveyor belts hauling disaster

Onto the waiting night barges. But we
Though we knew what had to be done,
Headed for the old lamb haunts,

Sheared the white lies off each other's backs,
Submerged in trout water to cleanse
Our bodies for the feast of deep touch.

And can you remember how our tongues
Rippled like mandolins and overhead
The fat whirring of mallard wings

And you as new as a baby hanging
From the umbilical and small flames
Running across the water and inland

Burning houses and we still in such
A frenzy to pick knowledge and bliss
From the vanishing paradise tree.

RICHARD TILLINGHAST

 Richard Tillinghast is a poet, translator and critic who was born in Memphis, Tennessee, in 1940 and now lives in Tipperary. He has published ten books of poetry including *The New Life*, 2008. His book of essays, *Finding Ireland: a Poet's Explorations of Irish Literature and Culture*, also came out in 2008. His poetry has appeared frequently in Irish, British, and American periodicals. Poems of his have been selected for both *The Best American Poetry* and *The Best of Irish Poetry*. Among his other books of essays is *Robert Lowell's Life and Work: Damaged Grandeur*, a critical memoir; Lowell was Tillinghast's teacher at Harvard. With his daughter, Julia Clare Tillinghast he has translated from Turkish the poems of Edip Cansever, to be launched in 2009. The Dedalus Press is also bringing out a Selected Poems in Ireland later this year. He has received grants from the American Research Institute in Turkey, the Arts Council of Ireland, the British Council, Harvard University, and the National Endowment for the Humanities. He is also the recipient of the Ann Stanford Prize and the James Dickey Prize, as well as the 2007 Cleanth Brooks Award for Creative Non-Fiction. In 2008 he was awarded an honorary Doctorate of Letters by The University of the South (Sewanee).

Rain

The rain, the incessant drench,
       the lap of it puddling up,
             seen through spattered window-glass.
And all of us in that long house together
       where all the talk was of the weather,
     house-partying on a rainy weekend.

Fragrance of toast, incessant cups of tea.
The wind mulled and hovered,
            the wind set all the buttercups in the field a-tremble.
I would sit all morning in the blue armchair transfixed,
                hearing the whoosh and settle of wind and rain
        surround and define
                    the astral shape of the cottage.

The rain was sleep till half past ten,
the rain was not having to shave,
the rain was opium,
the rain was an ocean voyage through blackness,
        a whisper under coverlets,
            a barely moving lace between ourselves and the trees.
The rain was constant, sempiternal, older than woodsmoke.

And then it would bow its head and subside,
        and a blackbird
tuning cleanly pinnacles of delight from a dry perch
                under dripping boughs
would put you in mind
of Noah and his lot
            drifting becalmed when the waters retreated.

I wanted it never to end.
I wanted to deconstitute and emanate out
            beyond the force-field of the cottage
        like lamplight through wet windows,
                and let the rain possess me entirely—
            let it soak right down
                into the pores of my happiness.

The World Is

The world is a man with big hands
and a mouth full of teeth.
The world is a ton of bricks, a busy signal,
your contempt for my small talk.
It's the crispy lace that hardens
around the egg you fry each morning
sunny side up.

The world is the last week of August,
the fumes that dizzy up into the heat
when you fill your tank
on the way to work late, again.
The world is "Please take a seat over there."
The world is "It'll have to come out."
The world is "Have a nice day."

The world is "What is that peculiar smell?"
The world is the button that popped off,
the watch that stopped, the lump you discover and turn on the light.
The world is a full ashtray, the world is that grey look,
the world is the County Coroner of Shelby County.
The world is a cortege of limousines,
an old man edging the grass from around a stone.

The world is "Ulster Says No!", the world is reliable
sources, a loud bang and shattered glass raining down on shoppers.
The world is a severed arm in a box of cabbages, "And then
the second bomb went off and we didn't know which
way to run." The world is Semtex and black balaclavas
and mouth-to-mouth resuscitation. The world is
car alarms silenced, and a street suddenly empty.

The world is one thousand dead today in the camps.
The world is sixty thousand latrines, the world is
bulldozers pushing bodies and parts of bodies into a ditch.
The world is dysentery and cholera,
infected blood, and vomit.
The world is mortality rates, and rape as an instrument of war.
  The world
is a 12-year-old with a Walkman, a can of Coke, and an Uzi.

The Emigrant

Two places only
there were:
here and America.
The four corners of the farm,
and gone-beyond-the-sea.

With a twopenny nail
he etched into the iron
shank of his spade
the word "Destiny",
drove it with his boot smartly into the earth
and left it standing.

Abroad commenced
at the town line.
The New World blinded him
on the Navan road
and again the first time he tried to speak English
and again the first time he saw an orange.

Anaesthetised by reels and barrels of porter
and eight renditions of "The Parting Glass",
he fell asleep to the groan of oars
and awoke to a diesel thrust
and sleet over mountainous seas.

Exilium

The imperial city toward which all roads tend,
Which codifies the laws and dispatches them
By runner or fax to expectant provinces
This is not. It's an improvised mélange
Mushrooming along the banks of a tidal river,
Suffering the moods of its irrational weather
And a population with much to complain about.

Though you could dignify what draws you here
By calling it exile, your solitude is your choice,
Even when it racks you, even when
Your tendons stretch with what you have to carry.
Out you go tonight making the rounds, mapping
A route through the city's drizzly melancholia
Down streets of broad colonial emptiness.

Step inside a stained glass door or two
Where shag and porter cloud the conversation.
Sip a slow pint in the company of strangers
While outside the rain slurs through globed lamp-glow.
The evening ages. A notebook fills with your
Idiosyncratic alphabet. Then the pubs close.

The pubs close, the streets rain-slick and desultory.
A cafeteria then—everybody's
Hangout, where plain lives put in appearances
Over tea and a bun. The cash register whirrs,
The steamy rush of the coffee machine backgrounds
A clink of ironstone plates and stainless steel.
No sign of leisure here: every life
In the room carries the imprint of having worked
The livelong day—not to boast or prove
A point, but simply because what else is there?

The way an old sufferer, grey hair wispy and thin,
Handles her knife, addressing a plate of fish,
Reaches you, touches some common chord.
Despite what they say about you—beyond your remoteness,
Your severe judgements on your fellow creatures—
You've some connection still to the human race.
Hypercritical, incommunicado,
It's good to know deep down you're one of us.

ERIKO TSUGAWA-MADDEN

 Eriko Tsugawa-Madden was born in Hokkaido, Japan. While travelling Europe in the 1980s, she decided to settle in Ireland and 2009 marked her twentieth year here. She was the first and only Japanese to have her poems short-listed for the Hennessy New Irish Writing Awards in 2003 and again in 2009. For as long as she can remember, she has been writing down her thoughts. She first moved into Stoneybatter in one of the oldest quarters of Dublin, where she was witness to many of the fading traditions associated with old Dublin. This inspired her to begin writing in English. Her poems have also been used in art publications in Japan. They are observations of nature, of people and also recollections of her Japanese childhood by the sea in remote Northern Japan. She has taught Japanese in University College Dublin and is an Irish National Guide. Eriko is married to an Irishman and has one son. She still lives in Dublin.

Typhoon

I learned to count when I was four.
I counted dead fishermen
Lined up on the sandy shore
Covered with straw mats.
Ichi...Ni...San...Shi...

I could count big numbers,
Pity there were only four.
I counted them
Like the shadows of fence-posts
I used to pass on the sandy hill.

I was told to stay at home
But I sneaked out the back door.
I saw them through the high marram
Grass on the dunes.

I counted fish washed ashore from the wrecked ship.
Salmon, Sea trout, Mackerel.
Ichi...Ni...San...Shi...
Some perfect, some not. Torn.
Villagers collected them in rusty buckets.
How many fish could I get?
I got none.

On the sandy hill
The grasses swelled and bent madly.
My skirt puffed.
The Sea was angry with me,
His mouth, teeth and tonsils,
Spitting foam, seething,
Exhausted by his own ill temper.

I shivered.

The ship's black belly rose and fell.
Stranded below the yellow cliffs.
Like a beached Whale.
Now breathing feebly.
Is he dying?

I started counting to his death.
Ichi...Ni...San...Shi...

These and those I counted.
After the Typhoon.

Chanteuse in the Shade

On Morning Star Avenue, I came across her.
She was sitting on her cardboard sofa
Leaning against the wall, in the shade
While I strolled.

'Why don't you move over there in the sun ?' said I.
The other side of the road, sunny & warm.
My suggestion meant nothing to her, but she
Shone herself, at being approached by a stranger.
She raised herself on her knees, to engage me.

Her eyes, full of eagerness to talk now.
'I once knew a China girl', she said.
'When I was a singer, in America'.
'Oh!, were you a singer?' I replied,
Still looking at the sunny side, hoping
She would move there.
'Oh, don't mention it. It's a long time ago.'

She talked about her cabaret career,
Her eyes straying skyward as the memories returned.
Then she started singing. Her throaty voice
Unexpectedly powerful for her skinny body.
While she sang, she swiftly licked her lips.
Her face lit up, without a spotlight.
I caught the smell of her whiskey breath.

Two men emerging from the Morning Star Hostel
Must have heard her singing, but passed on by.
A bottle of Paddy, peeped from her handbag,
Mingled with her other property. Her hand often
Moved towards it, but she pulled it back each time.

Oh, how bravely she sang on
Deprived of her warming fuel.
I left her alone on Morning Star Avenue
To continue my stroll towards Stoneybatter.
The sun now inching towards her.

Bell And Tree

My neighbour a retired man
Cut all the branches off a tree.
It stood there gnarled, a scarecrow.
He returned days later to cut the trunk
With a saw on a fine winter morning.
I stopped to talk.

'A variegated poplar, wasn't it?'
I remembered its new albino leaves
Like a colony of hatching moon moths
Fluttering in the slightest wind.
He rested the saw against the trunk
And his arm on an amputee branch.
'I haven't a clue about trees.
But someone had said it was maple.
If I remember rightly.' said he.

No – it's not maple, I thought to myself.
'You're working hard', I said instead.
'I could use a chainsaw, but I don't.
I have plenty of time.' said he.
His forehead shone slightly.

'Listen!' he said, looking up at the sky.
The church bell was ringing.
'It rings for the girl, did you know that?'
'No' I replied, tracing his gaze skywards
With my infidel eyes.

'A young girl killed herself.
She was suffering from depression.
She set herself on fire and died.
It's a terrible thing. This bell is for her.'

Eleven o'clock, the bell tolled for the girl.
An old man in his spare time kills a tree.
It was blocking out his sun, and he tells me
A young girl killed herself in a garden shed.
Now she has no time.
Who or what am I killing?

The bell must have been remarked upon by many.
Its stop will go unnoticed.

ROSE TUELO BROCK

 Rose Tuelo Brock was born in Mafikeng, South Africa, in 1939. After obtaining a Science Degree in 1962, she left her country to teach Science in a High school in Zimbabwe. There, she met her husband and they married in 1966. There followed years of teaching Science in various African countries including Kenya and Lesotho. In 1979, she, her husband and their two sons, arrived in Galway, Ireland. She worked as a part time lecturer in Physiology in the then Regional Technical College for some three years. After obtaining a Diploma for Community Development from University College, Galway, she embarked on a project to run, with others, a Development Education Resource Centre, The Galway 'One World' Centre. During this period, she gave talks and wrote essays on various subjects such as: age, gender, and race discrimination; the arms trade and its effects on parts of Africa; fair and just trade; world debt; difficulties and problems facing the so-called 'Third World', and other subjects. She also wrote short stories and poetry. From 1994 to 2009, she wrote a weekly column in the *Connacht City Tribune.*

Love

He loves me
Bruises, broken bones and black eye
Explained away to questioning looks.
Shame and fear are good controls.

She loves me, she belongs to me
To service me and me alone.
I will share her with nobody.

He loves me, it chokes me.
Through me his Merc, his BMW
And the best fashion are displayed.

She loves me.
She cannot do without my cash.
Like all my possessions,
She will do what, when and how I want.

He loves me
I am crippled and stripped.
Mind and body belong to him.
Is this it?

Trees of the Northern Winter

Tall, dominating, branches splayed,
The result of a search for the sun.
Like maidens, they are striking in their nudity.
Silently, they shout their power and beauty.

How I enjoy their complex simplicity
To have wings would be a blessing
Flit from tree to tree
Perch on the top tip surveying the world
And their quiet splendour.

Frost enhances their looks
As the bare branches display their frame,
White, majestic.

Trees of my youth were not so revealing
Year-long leafiness hid their hearts
Nests, even snakes, not so obvious.
Even as I relaxed in their generous shade
Plaiting hair or playing games
Their subtle seasonal response escaped me.

Flesh-Coloured

The cream failed to disguise the scar
Its pinkness emphasised the blemish
It joins such other purchases on the shelf
To remind me of moments of delusion

She recommends an item for wear
The colour is the selling point
Even as it is held close to my face
She fails to notice the clash in colour

Is mine not a flesh coloured skin?
One day, some maker might cop on.

ANDREAS VOGEL

Andreas Vogel was born in 1970 and grew up in the city of Bochum in Germany. He came to live in Conamara in 1996 were he is working with the educational organisation Muintearas. He started publishing poems in Irish in 2002 and his first collection *chomh gar 'gus is féidir—nicht näher* appeared from Coiscéim in 2009.

nicht Fisch nicht Fleisch

tá dúile is daoine coimhthíoch léi
is tá sí tuirseach de bheith ina maighdean mhara
go seasta ag aistriú ó mhuir go talamh
is ó thalamh go muir
ach ní thagann an dá thaobh le chéile
's fiú dá dtriomódh a hanam
's go ndéanfadh cré thur
cén sásamh a gheobhadh sí ó mhuintir na talún
an síor-ionadh céanna i súile gach éinne
is bíodh is go stánann na fir ar a cíocha
ní théann éinne i ngleic lena cairín éisc

nicht Fisch nicht Fleisch

both nature and mankind make strange with her
and she's sick and tired of being a mermaid
all the time switching from sea to land
is from land to sea

but the two will never be at one
and even if her soul dried up
and became shrivelled clay
she'd still get no joy from the folk of the land
only those looks of chronic wonder
the men might stare at her breasts alright
but no-one will tackle her fishy rump

(translated by the author)

Proinsias

bhris sé a mhéar nuair a bhuail sé
a dhorn ar mo ghiall

tá an ghráin aige orm

th'éis a bhfuil de chosáin ar an mbaile faoi le siúl
shílfeá gur mór leis mo lorg orthu

tá raithneach ag fás cois claí sa ngarraí bán

níor fhoghlaim sé mórán sa mbaile ná thall

strainséir é ina thírdhreach féin
rachadh coimhthíoch eile ina ghaobhar
thar a fhulaingt

ach siod é mo leiceann eile chuige

Proinsias

when he hit me in the jaw
he broke his finger

he can't stand me

all those paths he could go down
but he can't put up with the tracks I left

the fallow field is overgrown

he didn't learn much abroad or at home

he's a stranger in his own landscape
one more intruder
and he'll completely lose it

but wait till I let him feel my other cheek

(translated by the author)

MARIA WALLACE

Maria Wallace was born in Catalonia, in the early 1940s. Her parents were hillside farmers. When she was ten the family immigrated to Chile, where they lived for eight years. She came to Ireland in 1969 and married an Irishman. Since childhood she had felt the need to express creatively, first through drawing and painting, then through writing. The friction that her split loyalties, different background, culture and accent produces is her creative force. She has a B.A. in English and Spanish Literature, and an M.A. in Anglo-Irish Literature. Some of her work is influenced by Irish culture, traditions and folklore. Among her many awards is a Hennessy Literary Award, for poetry. Her work has appeared widely in newspapers, magazines and anthologies. She teaches languages, and facilitates a creative writing group. She edited the *Tallaght Soundings* anthology in 2007. A bilingual English / Catalan poetry collection appeared in 2009 in Barcelona.

An Bhoireann

You chose it. Named it.
Stony place belonging to
The people of Mruad.

All so long ago
Even the wind has forgotten
Which gods you worshipped, the way
You raised families,
Worked whatever land there was,
Watched over animals and marauding others,
Where you huddled against winter's ice.

In this sacred place, sometimes,
The heart may capture
Glimpses of you, echoes floating
In strange sounds. A complaining, a song
Of praise punctuated by the waves,
A lingering resonance,
Enunciations best understood
When left to the soul.

The World Around Me

The first thing I ever drew
Was my mother's face: a circle,
To me it was a circle,

With smaller ones inside:
Nose, eyes and mouth.

Later, I drew circles with legs,
And big feet for balance, arms
With big hands for all I could do
With them.

Sky and ground became two lines,
One above

One below;

In between not much for a while.

But, people began to ask *what's this*,
And *what's that* on the page.

I did not yet understand
About perimeters,
And saw a rich chain reaction
Of possibilities
In the way I re-created
The world around me.

I did not yet understand Paul Klee's
Take a line for a walk.

Today I do, and when I take one,
From time to time, it shows me the way.

The Meenybradden Bog Woman

*from the late medieval period, uncovered in 1978
in County Donegal*

Peat-brown hours
Turned to centuries,
Toughened
Your skin with the soft touch
Of nature's forgatherings.
A lullaby the drip and squelch
Of wet leavings,
The gossip of grasses,
The winnowing wind
And occasional birdsong
Rippling over you
Like the deepest, final note
Of a cello.
And you listening
To all that muted music,
Stilled in the hold of roots,

Under the brown-veined roof
Of your dark sky,

Hating the silent tongue
Of time.

Exchanging Essentials

My muse is male, an angel
Of light. When I'm blue
I sing lullabies to entice him
To my side, and whenever he plays
The lyre I pluck an upright quill
From his wing. *Heaven assigns*
Easier duties, he says playful.
He strokes
My words into the right angle
Of meaning, and between his thoughts
And mine, ink spills. As one
We have exchanged essentials,
Created new rhythms, made love
Patterns on paper, scores
Flowing from his wings of fantasy.
From his universe he brings
Lines I imprison, and in his hands
My rough outlines turn to
Calm eau de nil fields.

How long will this divine creature,
Limned in language, be mine?

I look into his eyes and know
He has stared at uncertainties
Longer than I.

CLIFF WEDGBURY

 Cliff Wedgbury is a Cork based poet, playwright, performing artist and broadcaster, born in London in 1946. His formative years were spent in the folk clubs, jazz clubs and second hand book shops of the Charing Cross Road area in London. He began writing during these years, and a selection of his work appeared at this time in an anthology published by the Greenwich Poetry Society. A Cloverdale competition prize winner in 1993, he saw publication in the United States of America, where his work was compared with the French poet, Jacques Prevert. His last collection *A Lingering Adolescence*, was published by Belfast Lapwing in 2007, and in October 2007 his poem *My Love Sold Revolutionary Newspapers* was included in the anthology *Che In Verse* (Aflame Books U.K) to acknowledge the 40th anniversary of the death of Che Guevara. He is also the composer of *The Ballad of Tom Crean*, and his CD *Antarctic Ballads* has been widely broadcast.

Brown Shoes

On the anniversary of my birth
I go back fifty years
and remember my late father
taking my hand and bringing me
to Mr Hannigan's shoe shop
Powis Street Woolwich 1953
the year the Queen was crowned
the year Everest was climbed
the year we installed a nine inch
black and white television
the year of our first caravan holiday to Dymchurch,
where grey bats flew across

the dark evening marshland
eels swam in deep black dykes
and the sea went all the way to France.

Though the war had been over for eight years
barbed wire and gun emplacements
littered the long shingle beaches
and the city bomb sights still remained
tomb stones to that sad conflict.

In Powis Street the scattered bricks were everywhere,
bleached skeletons long removed
but ghosts still lingering
as Dad told of shattered lives
and what we lose
when anger fills the hearts of men.

I held his warm hand
and walked in new brown shoes
across desolate bricks
on the afternoon of my seventh birthday.

Ant

I step on him by mistake,
not hearing
the shell-like body crunch.

I feel remorse
that such a busy little fellow
should be snubbed out so quickly
on his way to a hard day's work.

I look up at the sky guiltily,
awaiting the meteorite to fall,
remembering my father's death
running for the London train
and his unexpected call.

GRACE WELLS

Grace Wells was born in London, England in 1968. Formerly an independent television producer she moved to Ireland in 1991. Her first book, *Gyrfalcon* (The O'Brien Press, 2002), a novel for children, won the Eilís Dillon Best Newcomer Bisto Award, and was an International White Ravens' Choice. Subsequent publications for children include *Ice-Dreams* (The O'Brien Press 2008) and *One World, Our World* (Irish Aid, 2009). Her short stories and poetry have been published widely and broadcast on RTÉ. She reviews Irish poetry for *Contrary*, the University of Chicago's online literary journal, is a freelance arts administrator, and teaches creative writing. A committed environmentalist bewildered by the extreme make-over of Ireland's Tiger years, she is currently working on a first collection of poems, *When God has Been Called Away to Greater Things*.

The Funeral Director's Wife

Often I have watched his hands about a corpse,
the closing of the mouth like the closing of a tin can
gaping and wide; the jagged edge of memory
prevents a smoothing over.
He will conquer death, make of it a business;
dressed in ceremony his chiselled face
sets more stone-like with the years.

He doesn't know I sit with them.

The talk in whispers is of first kisses,
the way a loved one's lips turned sour in argument.
We share trinkets, baby hair kept tied in ribbon, flowers pressed

between the leaves of faint-ink letters
from sisters gone over the Atlantic at seventeen.
There is the telling of waking alone to the dark night
and of the shamings, teachers and fathers,
and I hold them, hold their passing, hold the dearest of things

while in the scrubbed yard he reverses the hearse.

The Dress

for Dave who owns the story

Remember how poor we were? The wolf curled
so tight at our door we tripped on it daily
until the stumble became a soft brush against fur, manageable,
its teeth a snarl of threat that never harmed
as if it had grown used to us, was glad
of the small scraps we threw from our table.

The children brought their own light, steady
as the glow of nightlamp burning by bunk-beds.
We were blessed; absent of brash modernity
they were quiet, curious—there was much
of you in them—and you
got down beside them to share their games.

What was left between us was thin, but fine
like the silk of the dress, so when we saw it that winter,
we recognised its cloth.
The street silent, dark but for the lit
window drawing us like moths. Your whisper
It was made for you. And it was.

Black folds that swung to the knee, scalloped shoulders,
the waist tailored to my own, a bodice
low enough to frame pale skin, breasts, beating heart;
I burned to wear it, Christmas coming
and my wardrobe shabby. Still I pulled you away,
Don't be daft, I'd never have the occasion.

It called into our dreams, crying down small lanes.
We heard it and couldn't sleep and bickered:
I burned food, dropped things, snapped at the children.
Even the wolf grew restless. Our soft days tarnished
until the relief when I saw it gone, lifted
from bare window, leaving me fit back into my life.

But what did you go without, sacrifice, bargain,
to make them wrap it in ribbon: you who didn't
have the money, nor I the occasion? Still, it looked well
about me when its time came and I stood shaking hands,
accepting condolences, offering the children
small comfort, as they lowered you into the earth.

Pioneer

The last memories of her husband have been sewn
into a quilt which barely warms her nights.
After bad dreams, their son and daughter sleep
furled beneath small flags of nightshirt
and brushed cotton sleeve worn thin of scent from use.
Four summers and their harsh winters
have passed since she marked his grave.
Her own parents write, begging her home,
begging, before the children run quite wild.

Formally, they offer a second cousin
with land near York, ask she seriously consider
this most suitable widower of some renown.
Their letters go unanswered.

She is loosely moored between two worlds,
anchored only by the children,
for all they have ever drunk is from the well of this place.
And what flows in her now
is rainwater, woodsmoke, silence reflected
on the lake surface; leaves turned,
hair snagged on briars. Stones. The small,
white feathers that line nests.
She is sung with fox bark and pheasant call.
Creatures roost in her thoughts, her days
are measured by the slink, the leap, the pounce,
the pitched balance of wings breaking into flight.
She too moves in feral ways.

And lavender soap on Sundays is a fine gauze veil,
though the men in church stare only with downcast eyes,
she knows what it is they smell on her, and wary of hunters,
she is afraid. She lives where the long road from town
meets the trackless purple mountains. Some nights
leaning into the silver shadows at her door
she wonders who will come for her first.
For the quiet is also pregnant with alcohol and laughter,
with a swagger some miles off, and there are eyes
that watch from the mauve shadow inland;
if she stood still long enough,
they would take her as one of their own tribe,
had she interest in belonging.

All she has carved for herself is a small square of land,
free of chickweed and scutch-grass, soil abundant with seed.

Tableau

First you will come upon your neighbour on the lane,
beneath elder blossom, above meadowsweet,
creamy hedges lining the way as if to a wedding;
aisles decked with ragged robin and loosestrife.

You will throw your arms around one another,
your broken heart breaking in the look upon her face,
you will cling and weep and say goodbye.
You are leaving the russet dog and the black kittens.

You have snapped roots to rip yourself from this ground.
No time for your roses, no matter their hunger
for your lips in spring, at your feet are suitcases
and small children scattered amidst them.

But everything is going to be well. You will
take the all-day coach, board the ferry at midnight.
The city and its empty pockets await you,
just as the taxi driver comes now to take your bag,

he is packing the trunk of the cab, he is driving
you away. Years later, thinking on those rounded
shoulders, the veined hands at the wheel,
you will see the great fold of wings beneath ordinary clothes,

you will recognize your angel.

SALLY WHEELER

Sally Wheeler was born in England in 1937 and went to the local co-educational grammar school, where the "Physics Lessons" took place. English was her best subject from early on; she adored stories and poems and soon began to write. She won a place at Somerville College, Oxford, where she took a first-class degree. She then worked for the Clarendon Press for two years on the New Supplement to the *Oxford English Dictionary*. While doing so, she met Marcus, who became her husband in 1960. In 1968 they came to Belfast when he was appointed Professor of Slavonic Studies at Queen's University. By the time her three children were older she started writing again, and in 1997 won the Brian Moore short story award. She had also begun writing poetry and joined the all-women's group 'Word of Mouth'. In 1996 they published an anthology *Word of Mouth* (Blackstaff Press, Belfast). Her own collection, *Mosaic*, was published by Summer Palace Press in 2004.

Physics Lessons

In double Physics time lay down and died.
We wrote out laws of a closed universe
where matter was transformed but never lost,
and all of solid-seeming visible nature,
including us, was made of atoms—least
of entities, and indivisible. Yet
we all knew the atom had been split,
making our future problematical;
and Einstein said that time did not exist
but all was one, in space, present and past.

We'd vaguely heard, though no one could explain
his idea, complex, mathematical.
To me, the theory had to do with trains
passing each other at a different rate.
From the lab we saw the mainline track,
and sometimes in those endless afternoons
the Physics master would get up and crane
out of the window, watch in hand, to check
The Flying Scot go hammering down the straight.
She's bang on time, he'd say, or *Slightly late*,
then sigh and put his watch away again.

Celebration

The city's ringed with fire;
rockets light up the sky,
new-coloured stars
below Orion's blaze.
We watch out in the cold,
two women with memories—
revived by sights like this—
of war, my country against hers.
I could see London in the blitz,
and she saw Hamburg in the raids.
Countdown to midnight; we embrace.
The year one minute old.
In the warm kitchen, where the radio plays
we swing each other in a waltz
around the table, half-
tipsy on champagne and Strauss;
How I regret, she says, *that in my life
I have not danced enough.*

Neighbours

Thirty years here—my longest anywhere;
children, small when we moved, one not yet born,
now all grown up and gone.
The garden where they played and washing blew
had trees and hedges to divide
us from our neighbours next door,
an elderly childless pair.
The wife, whom I never knew,
fell ill and died; her widower remained
and lived some years alone.
And then new neighbours came.
Their children fill the air
with noise and cries
just as ours did before;
and now, I realise,
we are to them
the elderly childless pair.
There's only one stage more.
Whichever of us survives
will turn into the one who lives
all on their own next door.

SABINE WICHERT

 Sabine Wichert was born in Graudenz, West Prussia (now Grudziadz, Poland) in 1942. She grew up in West Germany and was educated at various German and English universities. She taught history at Queen's University, Belfast from 1971 to 2007. From the late seventies she has written and published poems. Three collections of her poetry have appeared: *Tin Drum Country* (1995), *Sharing Darwin* (1999) and *Taganrog* (2004).

Black Box

'contemporary dwelling of last words'

Once upon a time there will be—
  a Queen, or not a Queen—
 a streetcar named forget,
   or remember,
 a dog named Tilly and
   a cat named Soraya—
children so well adjusted
  they will not fight their parents,
parents so confident they
  will not fight their children—
the weather predictable and
  the price of oil permanently low—
there will be stories about the past
  found in black boxes, open-ended,
  cut off in mid-sentence, mid-living:
nothing much to be proud of,
  mainly murder and mayhem—
a line will be drawn under the past:

the end of history, no more
looking for justification
of evil deeds in past evil deeds,
no more wars and pestilence,
no more where we came from—
there will only be continuous
presence, no more challenges, no more
obstacles, the tired pleasure of permanence.
Hope stepping over experience and
pushing it back into the black box.

The Newcomer

The dull grey of the stones and the bright green
of the ferns swaying with the wind and rain
remind her—

She once was that young girl at the traffic
lights, unaware of her beauty and what
age might do to her, or interested
in what configuration her future
life would fall, open only to living
and expectation—

When she'd lived in these parts well on twenty
years, longer than half her previous life and
longer than anywhere before, they said
it wouldn't do—

This place had solid roots in history
and even ten times twenty years would
still have seen her as a blow-in suspect.

Her mother had mothered her and later
she mothered her mother, both with a love
that expected little return, but gave
much affection and some consolation.

That evening when the wasps invaded
the cottage and they swatted them one by
one, between large gulps of wine, standing all
the time since there was only one chair—

On the day thereafter when they could not
take the boat because of inclement
weather and she watched it from upstairs for
half an hour ploughing through heavy sea on
route to the Skelligs, bouncing so much that
watching it made her dizzy—

Now she looks at all the old photos and
wonders: there's so much talk of closure, but
there's none to life, not even death—

Trying to Understand

M. looked at the book and said
uh, a history of Northern
Ireland. Yes, I nodded, and
glancing at the half-empty
lecture hall he added, pity
there aren't more; but I'm writing
one, I said, while scribbling at
a street plan I'd promised L.
When she arrived, M. said no,
I meant the audience, and
to L.: S. is writing a
poem on Northern Ireland.

LANDA WO

Landa Wo is an Angolan-French poet. Born in 1972 in Saint-Etienne (France) he is a graduate of the French education system. He was forced to leave his native country in 1999 for a ten-year exile, his status as one of the so-called "visible minorities" making it difficult for him to find work. Meanwhile, Yeats' Ireland had become the Celtic Tiger and offered more career opportunities to graduates, especially to those from a minority group who were denied them in France. Wo has used his writing both as a tool to integrate into Irish society, and as a weapon. He has won numerous awards such as 1st prize in Metro Éireann Writing Competition (2007), the Eist Poetry competition (2006), as well as 3rd place in the French section of the international poetry competition, Féile Filíochta (2005). His imagination is coloured by twenty years' experience of life lived in Gabon and in Congo. He is a member of the European Academy of Poetry.

Behind Tara Hill

To the dead of the hills

All the hills in the world
Keep terrible secrets.
When mankind lost his mind
In the swift killing of innocents,
This refugee boy left his home
With no other hope
Than to find his mother spirit
Behind Tara Hill.
I can still remember

The breath of his agony
In the early killing hours
Of this fresh Irish winter.
Every dead of the hills
From stomachs of wild animals
Seems to murmur to the boy:
Find our soul behind Tara Hill
And join us for a drink.

The Last Moabi

On his return from the hunt
The hunter put down his bag
On the red clay floor.
The weeping widow excused herself
For not having wood for the supper.
Fearing the anger of her husband
She burst into tears.
She showed him the last Moabi, to be cut down to make fire.
We will have a cold supper this evening he told her
Slowly closing the kitchen door.

Their Lips Move

Their lips move softly
To let escape a choked complaint
Their lips move gently
To unpick the seams of the wire tyranny
The dying cactus thinks about the Atlas oasis
Freedom of speech dances on the plain, on fire

Poet in exile

I am a poet in exile searching
For a new breath.
In the cold streets of my dreams
I meet the spirit of the revolution's exiles
I meet the word-hyenas
I meet a fine rain of dying October
I meet Sango words of lost vertigo
I meet a fire crouching by the shadow of time
I meet a dead beauty of Angola who reaches out to me.

I am a poet in exile searching
For a new breath
In the arms of the dead beauty of Abyssinia.
Hanging from her colourless hair
I travel on the back of a bitter comet
Ngondo Moyula[1] my ancestor
Ngondo Moyula the past in movement
Ngondo Moyula brother in destiny of the Caribbean Indians
May your murmur be the lullaby for my night with the dead
beauty of Niamey.

I am a poet in exile searching
For a new breath.
In the giant flames of a bush fire
The firefly-woman dances, her breasts free.
I plunge into the dark ravines of Amani
In search of the stone of passion
To break the lament of solitude.
My lips touch the lukewarm shoulder of the dead beauty of
Namibia
I abandon my body to pleasures of the night.

I am a poet in exile searching
For a new breath.
In the fleeting night
I make love with the dead beauty of Tanzania.
In passing I make her a gift of my petrified soul
I offer her my dreams, my hopes, my visions of the night
I murmur to her words stolen from the speechless Soko[2]
I give her the keys of time, the padlock of History.
The day is breaking; my lifeless body rests on a grave.

I am a poet in exile searching
For a new breath.
A parrot from paradise nests in my skull
The flicker from the Isle of Madagascar is joyful
He takes wing to spread the news of my death
Ngondo Moyula my ancestor
I inherited from you the fatal privilege of a night of Love
Give me a new breath to understand eternity.

1 Escaped convict from history
2 Tribe from the dense forest of Central Africa which inherited 1000 words at
the start of life. Everyone who dies takes 30 words to go and speak to the dead.
Each newborn arrives with one word. The Soko people will only find speech
again when the original 1000 words are reunited.

RACHEL AUDREY WYATT

 Born Rachel Hitchcock near Philadelphia, Pennsylvania, on the 23 September, 1970, Rachel Wyatt grew up in the United States. Having frequently relocated with her spouse and four children, she is living in Ireland for the second time. She returned to Dublin in 2003, where she is currently studying Arts at University College Dublin.

Nettles

Throughout my designs I find you threaded.
Snares curled tightly round deep stony anchors.
Beneath sweet fragrant flowers there concealed.
By brush of stinging silk, your weave betrayed.
Now laced intimate with all I've planted-
Side by side, their sheltering companion.
Soon when blossoms are remembered pleasures-
Such beauty here spent, withered on the stalk-
I will clothe me in your stronger fibres,
And drink your solace as the days grow dark.

Kite String

```
        spin    away
burn
        bare
                cool    space
tumble
        sway


                tug
full    taut    place

        circle                  slow
                        rise
                swell
        still bound


flutter
        low
                grace
sweep
        soft
ground
```

ADAM WYETH

 Adam Wyeth was born in Sussex, England, 1978. He was a prize winner of The Fish International Poetry Competition, 2009 and a runner-up of The Arvon International Poetry Competition, 2006. His poems have been anthologized in *The Best of Irish Poetry* anthology, 2010, *Something Beginning with P* and The *Arvon 25th Anniversary* Anthology. His work has appeared in numerous literary journals, including, *The Stinging Fly, The SHOp, Southword, Poetry London and Magma.* He was a featured poet in *Agenda* and selected for the Poetry Ireland Introductions Series, 2007. He has made two films on poetry, *A Life in the Day of Desmond O'Grady,* first screened at The Cork Film Festival, 2004; and a full length feature, *Soundeye: Cork International Poetry Festival, 2005.* He runs various Creative Writing and Poetry Appreciation workshops and is a member of the Poetry Ireland Writers in Schools Scheme. He lives in Co. Cork.

Google Earth

> *The poet's eye, in fine frenzy rolling,*
> *Doth glance from heaven to earth, from earth to heaven.*
>   *—Theseus from A Midsummer Night's Dream*
>   *Act V, Scene 1*

We started in Africa, the world at our fingertips,
dropped in on your house in Zimbabwe; threading
our way north out of Harare into the suburbs,
magnifying the streets—*the forms of things unknown,*
till we spotted your mum's white Mercedes parked
in the driveway; seeming—*more strange than true,*

the three of us huddled round a monitor in Streatham,
you pointed out the swimming pool and stables.
We whizzed out, looking down on our blue planet,
then like gods—zoomed in towards Ireland—
taking the road west from Cork to Kinsale,
following the Bandon river through Innishannon,
turning off and leapfrogging over farms
to find our home framed in fields of barley;
enlarged the display to see our sycamore's leaves
waving back. Then with the touch of a button,
we were smack bang in Central London,
tracing our footsteps earlier in the day, walking
the wobbly bridge between St Paul's and Tate Modern;
the London Eye staring majestically over the Thames.
South through Brixton into Streatham—
one sees more devils than vast hell can hold—
the blank expressions of millions of roofs gazing
squarely up at us, while we made our way down
the avenue, as if we were trying to sneak up
on ourselves; till there we were right outside the door:
the lunatic, the lover and the poet—peeping through
the computer screen like a window to our souls.

Oxbow Lake

From Lesotho to Sullivan's Quay,
Maurice Scully inscribed in his book
of poetry to me. Because I caught
wind of him mentioning a Basotho blanket
in one of his poems. We got
talking—how we both went to Lesotho:
seeking adventure, growing our hair.

And we ran through places
we visited there, like a river snaking down
the mountains, till our paths
criss-crossed here—converging
like an oxbow lake. From The Kingdom in the Sky
to the People's Republic of Cork
below the sea. And under his signature
X marked the spot to me.

X marked the spot to me
below the sea, and under his signature,
to the People's Republic of Cork.
Like an oxbow lake from The Kingdom in the Sky,
criss-crossed here—converging
the mountains. Till our paths
we visited there, like a river snaking down.
And we ran through places,
seeking adventure, growing our hair.
Talking—how we both went to Lesotho
in one of his poems. We got
wind of him mentioning a Basotho blanket
of poetry to me. Because I caught
Maurice Scully—inscribed in his book,
From Lesotho to Sullivan's Quay.

A Viking Comes to Tea

He didn't knock, rammed through the door, ranting
and raving in old Norse. Sniffed about the place—
then, gathering pieces of debris, proceeded
to make a fire in the middle of the room.
I had cream and jam scones all prepared,

but knew he'd be happier gnawing on the dog's bone.
He didn't speak much, what with the language
barrier; mostly murmurs and grunts, belches
whilst chewing, and bellows before he downed
in one—the pot of tea. When it scorched
his throat and insides I thought his horns
would really show, but au contraire—
after his face went scarlet and he roared
like thunder, pummelling his belly like a drum,
he became strangely calm.
And beneath the forest of oleaginous whiskers
I detected a faint smile. He began stroking
my hair and feeling the fabric of my dress.
So I took him upstairs and showed him
my garments. He loved bright colours
but most of all he loved the softness.
I brushed out his plaits, shaved his beard
and ran a hot bath. I prepared dinner:
moules mariniere, followed by sauté chicken,
ending with crème brulee. He looked like a princess
as he came down in my wedding dress.
I showed him how to eat delicately.
Then after coffee—listening to Mozart—
the beast in *me* guided his hand.

ALEX WYLIE

 Alex Wylie was born in Blackpool, England in 1980, his father English, his mother Maltese. He studied literature at the Universities of Central Lancashire and Durham before moving to Belfast to write a doctoral thesis on poetry at Queen's University, which he completed last year. He has published poetry, reviews and essays in various magazines and journals, and is currently 'working towards a first collection'. He has lived in Belfast for some five years.

Revisiting the Forge

They've given us a clue: the sound
of hammers clanging into anvils is an echo
of angelic harmony. I heard it on the radio.
According to the experts, around
520 BC a scientist
hesitated by a smithy door—slumming
it like a king in furs—
at a moment of personal crisis
impossible music, spirit's blood-beat, drumming
down a harmony of spheres

(meanwhile the nameless blacksmith hears
a scraping at the door, looks up and hits his thumb
and screams blue murder. Pythagoras, struck dumb
in sunlight, invents the music of the spheres).

The Venus Lander

Thirty-five million miles of nothingness
to go, five million gone, I dream in darkness
of your skies, your sulphur, wings spread to address

the sun; balanced, for a time, in space
great minds have wandered behind screwed-up eyes,
or theorized as heaven, or dreamed of monsters

gnawing the bones of heaven as they fell.
Each day transmits me further—mechanical
half-dinosaur—closer, closer to the unreal

I was made for. And if expiry is rebirth
when the brain has burned out, and I am myth,
I will solve, forever, the riddles of your earth.

A Baroque Ceiling

(Rubens, Whitehall Banqueting House)

They had it all, those rampant cavaliers
Brought out of limbo back to English life,

And knew it all too well; whose art proclaims
The age in redolence of sex and war,

In superhuman marble and in ceilings
Covering the white earth with skies of louche.

History a pageant, the mind its own place
As here, on high, two women struggle

In symbolic lust—one beautiful, the other foul
To look on, the one trampling the other

In the artist's vision of servility—
Avarice and Bounty, bare-armed for war,

Tumbling forever into England.

Tableau Parisien

Pascal, delirious, ices his glass
With a clatter that echoes down the Rue Montparnasse

Between his ears: pours the cognac: grips
The needle: injects his nervous fingertips

With you-know-what for damnable relief.
 The room agog with *objets primitif*

Like a bustling crowd at noon; the riot
Of day followed by the ringing quiet

Of night. Only a soulful cat miaows
At the bourgeois double-chinned chateaus

As Pascal waits, the brandy-coloured flame
Beating like fever through the shut room

Of his heart, for the spirit to come
With cold hands to chill out his delirium—

Ice-perfect, of Paradise
Immaculate and melting eyes—

Wings outstretched, dripping the carpet
Like stalactites. As if a parapet

Of cloud (not Pascal's apartment
In the 2e *arrondissement*)

Were where they were, her clear appeal
A surface deadened fingertips could feel,

She sings: Between ourselves—you there,
Me here, *bien de chair, mon cher*—

...

A river runs, broken with a weight
Of oil on its slender water

Unmoved by driftage or disruptive weather;
A plague upon the birds that fight

Beneath its trees, invading their shelter
Like the smoke of waste-fires. From my height

It's rainbows' blood; from yours, it's ion, nitrate;
The carbon footprint of the average commuter

Slipped from the leaky shoe of a tourist-boat;
A picture changed with every changing colour

Dispersing like unwanted news, and sunlight
Pixellated on a screen of water.

And ice that fleshed the river
Disintegrates forever...

...

Riddled with sleep, Pascal stirs
The cognac with his perforated fingers,

Observes the ice therein: cold ichor
Sinking through the burning flesh of liquor

Like spirit slumping in its blood.
And like a mischief-making stable-lad

Sent home for good, lets bolt his thought
Then stands, oblivious to his gout,

In the pool of the angel a moment ago.
Mindless. Pure as the driven snow.

ANN ZELL

 Ann Zell was born in 1933 and grew up with many brothers on a dirt farm in southeastern Idaho, USA. Since leaving home to attend university, she has lived in Utah, California, New York, Spain, and London, moving to Ireland in 1980 and settling in West Belfast, where she worked for a number of years at the Royal Victoria Hospital as a medical secretary. Much of her adult energy has been directed to radical politics. She began writing poetry seriously in her mid-fifties, has published two collections (*Weathering*, Salmon Press and *Between Me and All Harm*, Summer Palace Press), and is working on a third. She is a founder member of the Word of Mouth Poetry Collective, a group of women poets who meet regularly in Belfast to critique one another's poems, and promote poetry to audiences throughout Ireland

Rainy Day Bus

All us
        oldies with passes
                and mothers with push chairs
                        are wet through.

The bus judders and groans around
the only / impossible
corner

curtsies at the pick-up point
where another push chair gets on

hiccups and belches
through three traffic lights
within a couple of hundred yards
and gathers breath on Divis Street
for the jounce up the Falls.

A wild way to travel.
Finessing the brakes
is not taught on the PSV Driving Course.
The danger is part of the fun.

Sat in the only seat with
                          nothing to grab onto
I admire the back view
of the mountainy man in a flat cap and blue tweed jacket
who won the game of *after you Alphonse, after you Gaston*
and made me get on first.

A woman with too many messages
sways alarming-
                ly
on thin legs encased in tissue-paper skin

but won't sit   (although we offer her seats)
because she's getting off at the next stop.

It's turned out a terrible morning.

        (temperature's dropped 10 degrees
        and the storm's sweeping in)

Yup, I agree, grinning.

The summer of ...

for Ruth

How could I ignore swallows for so many years?

This summer, they're everywhere—

skimming the stepped grass around the cathedral,
teasing a friend's dog with their garden swoops

sharing the higher air with the squadrons of swifts
whose screams alert you to look up now!

Blink, and they're gone,
leaving a trail of sparklers behind the eye.

And except for the pleasure you get,
following their roller-coaster flight
there's no need to track what crosses this sky.

Returning

Coming down from Salmon River Country
where my father dreams of a cattle ranch

through the cut-up hills of the Lemhi Valley
and the Snake River plain where nobody lives

to the first haphazard, weatherbeaten
houses—harrows and rakes in the bare yards.

Rows of sugar beets and potatoes
planted perpendicular to the road

open like the ribs of a giant fan
as we spin past in the station wagon

sunburnt and hungry, kicking each other
to relieve the ache from sitting still too long.

(We're wobbling out of control; the gravity
of our father's threats is too weak

to hold us in orbit; all of us know
he has to get home to the waiting cows.)

Crossing the Snake, muddy and high,
running so fast a child could be swept away

to Idaho Falls . . . Twin Falls . . . American
Falls . . . the Columbia . . . the Ocean.

Past the sod house dug into a bank,
the turn-offs for Berretts, Fulmers, Pooles

over the canal and down the driveway
to the fresh insult of the cow corral

the shimmering windbreak of Russian olives,
the lawn our city mother insisted on.

At supper, under the milk-glass globe,
I break buttered toast into tomato soup

adding planets of melted butter
to the sun reflected in an orange sky.

Excursion

Diminuendo of repeated forms,
tracks regressing to infinity
revive my panic dream of
a train that may or may not come.

On the nastiest
day of the year so far
I'm waiting at Dundalk Station
for the Belfast train back home

sitting on one of four pine chairs
around an oval table
in the Ladies' Waiting Room
where no Ladies wait

surrounded by monochrome
photos of railwaymen
the days when a body could go
from Greenore to Donegal

and full colour posters
with questions in four languages
aimed at other women
who must have travelled here in hope.

I answer in their absence
according to my circumstances.
As birth and class and
luck would have it

nyet, I am not a sex slave
nu, I am not being trafficked
non, I am not a victim
bu shi, I am not in fear.

ABOUT THE EDITORS

 Eva Bourke has published five collections of poetry, most recently *The Latitude of Naples* (Dedalus, 2005). Her *New and Selected Poems* are due in 2011. She has published several books of translations of Irish and German poets and is currently completing the translations for an anthology of German poetry of the 20th and 21st century, also to be published by Dedalus. Eva Bourke has read at festivals all over Europe, the US and Central America. Her work has been translated into many languages, and she has lectured on poetry and taught creative writing at universities in the United States and Ireland. She has received numerous awards and bursaries from the Arts Council and is a member of Aosdána, Ireland's academy of artists and writers.

 **Borbála Faragó** was born in Budapest. She studied English in Eötvös Loránd University, Budapest, and moved to Ireland in 1997. She completed her PhD in University College, Dublin in 2006 and is currently preparing a monograph on the poetry of Medbh McGuckian. She is the co-editor of *Facing The Other: Interdisciplinary Studies on Race, Gender and Social Justice in Ireland* (2008), and the author of numerous articles on contemporary Irish poetry. She lives in Dublin with her husband and three children.

Dedalus Press
Poetry from Ireland and the world

Established in 1985, the Dedalus Press is one of
Ireland's best-known literary imprints, dedicated
to new Irish poetry and to poetry from around the
world in English translation.

For further information on Dedalus Press titles, or
to visit our Audio Room of free-to-download
recordings by many of the poets on our list, see

www.dedaluspress.com

Lightning Source UK Ltd.
Milton Keynes UK
26 January 2010

149149UK00001B/2/P